1-12-91

7:45 pm

9/94 WND 8/94 ZIT
4/96 " 6/95 29T

COOKING WITH
Bon Appétit

COOKING WITH
Bon Appétit

Cookies

THE KNAPP PRESS
Publishers
Los Angeles

Library of Congress Cataloging in Publication Data

Main entry under title:

Cookies.

  (Cooking with Bon appétit)
  Recipes from Bon appétit magazine.
  1. Cookies. I. Bon appétit. II. Series.
TX772.C639 1987   641.8′654   86-27192
ISBN 0-89535-178-1

On the cover: *Thumbprint Poppy Seed Cookies. Photo by Peter Högg.*

❦ Contents

❧ *Foreword*

Cookies are a universal treat. Practically every country has its traditional favorites, whether it's Italian biscotti, German lebkuchen or French madeleines. And who can deny the irresistible appeal of all-American chocolate chip cookies or nut-studded brownies?

All cookies are basically quite simple and easy to make. But the delightful variety of ingredients and preparation methods makes them endlessly interesting and fun. They're the perfect choice for a light dessert, for afternoon tea, special-occasion gifts—or any time you want a quick and delicious snack.

In this collection of more than 200 of *Bon Appétit*'s most tempting cookies, we've pulled together some great international recipes as well as family favorites. The first four chapters are organized by method of preparation: drop cookies; hand-shaped and refrigerator cookies; rolled cookies; and bars and brownies. Fancy ones and those requiring special equipment have been assembled into the chapter on specialty cookies. Small pastries are included in the last chapter. In addition, throughout the book you'll find information boxes to help you make the best cookie you've ever eaten: "Pointers for Perfect Cookies" (page 15) and "Macaroons" (page 67).

Cookies are the original convenience dessert. Many of the doughs can be refrigerated or frozen, so you can keep them on hand, ready to be sliced and baked whenever you need a quick treat. And once baked, most cookies can be stored for several weeks at room temperature or frozen for several months. When storing them, be sure to pack different kinds separately so they retain their individual flavors. Separate each layer with waxed paper or parchment paper, and store the cookies in a box or tin or a wrapping of double-thickness aluminum foil.

No matter what the occasion, whether it's something fancy for an elegant dinner party, a hearty holiday pastry or just a simple, wholesome family treat, you will find a wealth of selections here to satisfy even the most discriminating cookie monster.

1 ❦ Drop Cookies

Drop cookies are among the simplest to make. All the recipes in this chapter involve the same basic procedure: a spoonful of prepared dough (an equal amount each time to ensure uniform baking) is dropped (usually with the help of another spoon), onto a cookie sheet and baked.

In spite of this ease in preparation, drop cookies come in an incredible array of guises. There is one to please everyone. Double Chocolate Cookies (page 2), crisp on the outside and fudgy within, will delight chocolate lovers. Maple Pecan Lace Cookies (page 4) are the perfect sweet accompaniment to fresh fruit, sorbet or ice cream. Butter cookies abound in this chapter, from the best-ever basic one (page 7) to a terrific lemon-glazed version (page 7). Wholesome rolled oats, cereal and your choice of coconut, chocolate chips, raisins or nuts pack Ranger Cookies (page 11) with lots of energy potential. For something out of the ordinary, try the Chinese Noodle Cookies (page 14), a unique combination of peanut butter chips, crisp chow mein noodles, pecans and marshmallows. The bonus here? Their microwave "baking" saves even more time for the busy cook.

Mocha Chocolate Chip Cookies

Makes about 7 dozen

3 cups semisweet chocolate chips
$^1/_2$ cup (1 stick) butter
4 ounces unsweetened chocolate

$^1/_2$ cup all purpose flour
$^1/_2$ teaspoon baking powder
$^1/_2$ teaspoon salt

4 eggs, room temperature
$1^1/_2$ cups sugar
$1^1/_2$ tablespoons instant coffee powder
2 teaspoons vanilla

Melt $1^1/_2$ cups chocolate chips, butter and unsweetened chocolate in top of double boiler set over hot (but not boiling) water. Stir until smooth. Remove from over water.

Preheat oven to 350°F. Line baking sheets with parchment or waxed paper. Combine flour, baking powder and salt. Beat eggs, sugar, coffee powder and vanilla in large bowl of electric mixer at high speed 2 minutes. Stir in chocolate mixture, then flour. Add remaining $1^1/_2$ cups chocolate chips. Drop batter onto prepared sheets by teaspoons, spacing evenly. Bake until cookies are crackled and shiny outside but still soft inside, about 8 minutes; do not overbake. Cool completely before removing from sheets. Store in airtight container.

For variation, add 2 cups chopped toasted pecans to batter.

Double Chocolate Cookies

This old-fashioned cookie is crisp on the outside and fudgy within.

Makes about 3 dozen 3-inch cookies.

5 ounces sweet chocolate, broken into pieces
$^1/_2$ cup firmly packed dark brown sugar
$^1/_2$ cup sugar
$^1/_2$ cup (1 stick) unsalted butter, cut into 4 pieces, room temperature
1 egg
2 teaspoons vanilla

1 cup minus 2 tablespoons unbleached all purpose flour
$^1/_2$ teaspoon baking soda
Pinch of salt
1 cup semisweet chocolate chips (6 ounces)
$^1/_2$ cup pecan halves or pieces

Position rack in center of oven and then preheat to 350°F.

Combine chocolate and sugars in processor work bowl and chop using 6 on/off turns, then process until chocolate is as fine as sugar, about 1 minute, stopping as necessary to scrape down sides and cover of work bowl. Add butter and blend 30 seconds. Add egg and vanilla and blend 1 minute, stopping as necessary to scrape down sides of work bowl. Add flour, baking soda and salt. Top with chocolate chips and pecans and mix using 2 on/off turns. Run spatula around inside of work bowl to loosen mixture. Blend again using 2 on/off turns.

Drop batter by slightly rounded tablespoons onto ungreased baking sheet, spacing $1^1/_2$ inches apart. Bake 10 minutes. Cool 3 minutes on baking sheet. Transfer to racks to cool completely.

Jody and Danielle's Double Chip Cookies

Makes 6 dozen

Butter
1 cup (2 sticks) butter, room
    temperature
1 cup chunky peanut butter
1 cup sugar
1 cup firmly packed brown sugar
2 eggs, beaten to blend

2 cups all purpose flour
1 teaspoon baking soda
1 6-ounce package semisweet
    chocolate chips
1 6-ounce package peanut butter
    chips

Preheat oven to 325°F. Butter baking sheets. Using electric mixer, cream 1 cup butter with peanut butter. Gradually beat in sugars and eggs until smooth. Beat in flour and baking soda until well blended. Stir in chocolate and peanut butter chips. Drop by rounded teaspoonfuls onto prepared sheets, spacing 2 inches apart. Flatten cookies slightly with fork. Bake until golden, 12 to 15 minutes. Cool completely on racks.

Chocolate Hazelnut Cookies (Brutti ma Buoni al Cacoa)

Makes about 28

3 egg whites, room temperature
1¹/₂ cups sugar
1 cup plus 1 tablespoon
    unsweetened cocoa powder

1¹/₄ cups hazelnuts, toasted, husked
    and coarsely chopped

Preheat oven to 300°F. Line baking sheet with parchment paper. Using electric mixer, beat whites until soft peaks form. Gradually add sugar and beat until stiff and shiny. Stir in cocoa powder. Fold in hazelnuts. Transfer to heavy large saucepan. Set over medium heat and stir with wooden spoon until mixture is shiny and pulls away from bottom and sides of pan, about 6 minutes. Drop batter by teaspoonfuls onto prepared sheet. Bake until firm, about 25 minutes.

Chocolate Chip Meringues

Makes about 4 dozen

3 egg whites
Pinch of salt
1 cup sugar
1 6-ounce package semisweet
    chocolate chips

2 tablespoons unsweetened cocoa
    powder
¹/₂ teaspoon vanilla

Preheat oven to 275°F. Line baking sheets with foil. Beat egg whites with salt until stiff. Gradually beat in sugar. Stir in chocolate chips, cocoa powder and vanilla. Drop batter by walnut-sized spoonfuls onto prepared sheets. Bake 30 minutes. Transfer entire foil sheet to rack and allow cookies to cool. Store in airtight container.

Fantasy Fudge Cookies

Makes about 5 dozen

1 cup (2 sticks) butter, room
temperature
1¹/₂ cups sugar
2 eggs, room temperature
1 teaspoon vanilla
2 cups all purpose flour
²/₃ cup unsweetened cocoa powder

³/₄ teaspoon baking soda
¹/₂ teaspoon salt
1 8-ounce package Reese's Pieces
candy
¹/₄ cup semisweet chocolate chips

Preheat oven to 350°F. Lightly grease baking sheets. Cream butter with sugar in large bowl. Blend in eggs 1 at a time. Stir in vanilla. Combine flour, cocoa powder, baking soda and salt. Slowly beat into creamed mixture. Stir in candy and chocolate chips. Drop dough by teaspoonfuls onto prepared sheets, spacing 2 inches apart. Bake until set, but still very soft, 10 to 12 minutes. (Cookies will firm as they cool.) Transfer to racks to cool completely.

Fudgy Potato Drops

Makes 6 dozen

Fudge Frosting
6 tablespoons (³/₄ stick) butter
1¹/₂ ounces unsweetened chocolate
4¹/₂ tablespoons milk, room
temperature
3 cups powdered sugar (³/₄ pound)
³/₄ teaspoon vanilla

¹/₄ cup solid vegetable shortening
1 cup firmly packed brown sugar
¹/₂ cup cold mashed potatoes
1 egg

2 ounces unsweetened chocolate,
melted
1 teaspoon vanilla
1¹/₂ cups all purpose flour
¹/₂ teaspoon salt
¹/₂ teaspoon baking soda
³/₄ cup buttermilk
¹/₂ cup chopped pecans, toasted
Pecan halves (optional)

For frosting: Melt butter and chocolate in small saucepan over low heat. Transfer to bowl. Add milk and stir until smooth. Beat in sugar and vanilla and blend thoroughly. Cover and set aside.

Preheat oven to 400°F. Grease baking sheets. Cream shortening with sugar in large mixing bowl. Beat in potatoes, egg, chocolate and vanilla and mix thoroughly. Sift flour, salt and baking soda. Blend into potato mixture alternately with buttermilk. Stir in chopped pecans. Drop dough onto prepared sheets by heaping teaspoons, spacing 2 inches apart. Bake until browned, about 6 to 8 minutes. Cool on rack 5 minutes. Spread 1¹/₂ teaspoons frosting over each cookie while warm. Press pecan half into top.

Maple Pecan Lace Cookies

Makes about 40

¹/₂ cup (1 stick) butter, room
temperature
1 cup firmly packed light brown
sugar
1 egg
1 teaspoon maple extract

¹/₂ cup sifted all purpose flour
1 teaspoon baking powder
¹/₂ teaspoon salt
²/₃ cup finely chopped pecans

Position rack in center of oven and preheat to 400°F. Lightly grease baking sheets. Cream butter with sugar. Beat in egg and maple extract. Sift flour, baking powder and salt into butter mixture. Blend until well combined. Stir in pecans. Drop batter by teaspoon onto prepared sheets, spacing 2 inches apart. Bake until cookies brown around edges and begin to brown in centers, about 6 minutes. Cool 2 minutes. Transfer to rack and cool. Store in airtight container.

Lacy Hazelnut Cookies (Palets aux Noisettes)

Makes about 6 dozen

1¼ cups chopped hazelnuts (about ⅓ pound)
⅔ cup sugar
3 tablespoons all purpose flour
1 tablespoon cornstarch
Pinch of salt

3 tablespoons butter, melted and cooled
1 teaspoon vanilla
1 teaspoon cinnamon
3 egg whites

Mix hazelnuts, sugar, flour, cornstarch and salt in large bowl. Blend butter, vanilla and cinnamon in small bowl. Add butter mixture to hazelnut mixture and blend well. Add whites and mix until smooth. Chill 30 minutes.

Preheat oven to 400°F. Line baking sheet with foil. Drop batter onto prepared baking sheet by half teaspoons, spacing 2 inches apart. Dip small metal spatula into cold water. Spread cookies to width of 1¼ inches, moistening spatula for each cookie. Bake until cookies are deep golden and 2 inches wide, about 7 to 8 minutes. Transfer to rack using spatula. Cool before serving. (*Cookies can be prepared 1 week ahead and stored airtight at room temperature.*)

Pecan Wafers

Sandwich these delicate, crisp cookies with ganache or dip in chocolate for a more elegant presentation.

Makes about 5 dozen

1 cup (2 sticks) unsalted butter, room temperature
1 cup sugar
2 egg whites, room temperature
1 pound pecans, toasted and finely ground

¼ cup all purpose flour
¼ teaspoon salt

Preheat oven to 350°F. Lightly grease baking sheets. Using electric mixer, cream butter until light. Add sugar and beat until light and fluffy. Add whites 1 at a time, beating until smooth paste forms. Combine pecans, flour and salt. Using spoon, fold into batter. Spoon batter onto prepared sheets by rounded teaspoonfuls, spacing 2 inches apart. Bake until cookies are golden brown, about 10 minutes. Cool on rack. (*Can be prepared 1 day ahead. Store in airtight container.*)

Lacy Oatmeal Cookies

Makes about 5 dozen

1/2 cup (1 stick) butter, melted
1 1/2 cups quick-cooking oats
3/4 cup sugar
1 egg, beaten to blend
2 teaspoons vanilla

1 teaspoon all purpose flour
1 teaspoon baking powder
1/2 teaspoon salt
1 2 1/2-ounce package walnuts, finely chopped

Preheat oven to 375°F. Line baking sheet with foil. Pour melted butter over oats in large bowl. Toss with fork. Stir in sugar. Add egg, vanilla, flour, baking powder and salt. Stir in walnuts. Drop onto prepared sheet by level teaspoons, spacing 2 inches apart. Bake until lightly browned, about 10 minutes. Cool on sheet. Gently peel cookies off foil. Arrange in layers in airtight container.

Ann's Lace Cookies

Makes about 40

2/3 cup firmly packed brown sugar
1/2 cup (1 stick) butter
1/2 cup light corn syrup

1 cup all purpose flour
3/4 cup chopped walnuts

Preheat oven to 325°F. Combine sugar, butter and syrup in small saucepan and blend well. Place over medium heat and bring to boil. Remove from heat and immediately stir in flour and nuts, blending well. Drop by teaspoonfuls onto baking sheet. Bake until set, about 8 to 10 minutes. Quickly remove from baking sheet and let cool on racks.

Orange Wafers (Gallettine all'Arancia)

Lacy rounds that are a cross between a cookie and a candy. They tend to soften at room temperature but stay crisp if stored in the freezer.

Makes about 3 dozen

3/4 cup unblanched almonds
1/2 cup coarsely chopped Glacéed Orange Peel*
3 tablespoons unsalted butter
1/3 cup sugar

1/4 cup whipping cream
1 tablespoon orange liqueur
Pinch of salt
2 tablespoons all purpose flour

Preheat oven to 375°F. Line baking sheets with parchment. Finely chop almonds and orange peel in processor. Melt butter with sugar and cream in heavy small saucepan over low heat, stirring frequently. Increase heat to medium-high and bring to boil. Remove from heat and stir in almond mixture, liqueur and salt. Stir in flour until batter is just blended.

Drop mixture by teaspoons onto prepared sheets, spacing 2 inches apart. Spread evenly to 1/8-inch-thick rounds using knife. Bake cookies until golden brown, 10 to 12 minutes. Transfer parchment with cookies to rack. Let stand until almost cool, then peel cookies from parchment. Cool completely on racks. Store in freezer in airtight container. Serve cold.

*Glacéed Orange Peel

Makes about 1 pound

4 large oranges, washed
12 cups water

1 3/4 cups water

1 1/2 cups sugar
1/2 cup honey

Score oranges into quarters; remove peel with any white pith that clings to it. (Reserve oranges for another use.) Cut peel into 3/8-inch-wide strips. Boil with 6 cups water in heavy large saucepan 10 minutes. Drain. Repeat with 6 cups fresh water. Drain well.

Combine 1 3/4 cups water, sugar and honey in same saucepan. Heat over low heat, swirling pan occasionally, until sugar dissolves. Increase heat and bring to boil. Mix in peel. Boil gently until peel is tender and syrup is reduced to 3/4 cup, stirring frequently, about 40 minutes. Cool in colander, stirring occasionally. Store in airtight container. (*Can be refrigerated up to 2 months.*)

Basic Butter Cookies

Makes about 30 cookies

1 cup all purpose flour
1/2 cup cornstarch
1/2 cup powdered sugar
3/4 cup (1 1/2 sticks) butter, room temperature

1/2 cup coarsely chopped or sliced walnuts

Preheat oven to 300°F. Sift first 3 ingredients into large bowl. Add butter and mix well. Stir in walnuts. Drop by teaspoons onto baking sheet. Bake until cookies are lightly golden, 20 to 25 minutes. Cool on racks.

Chocolate chips, toasted coconut, raisins, granola or chopped dates can be substituted for walnuts.

Lemon-Glazed Butter Cookies

Makes 3 dozen

1 cup (2 sticks) unsalted butter, room temperature
1/3 cup powdered sugar
1 cup all purpose flour
2/3 cup cornstarch

2 1/2 cups powdered sugar, sifted
1/2 cup (1 stick) butter, melted
2 tablespoons fresh lemon juice

Preheat oven to 350°F. Using electric mixer, beat butter and 1/3 cup sugar on medium speed 1 minute. Sift together flour and cornstarch. Add to butter. Blend until dough is soft, about 1 minute. Drop by teaspoonfuls onto ungreased baking sheet. Bake until very lightly browned, about 15 minutes. Transfer cookies to racks to cool.

Meanwhile, combine 2 1/2 cups sugar, melted butter and lemon juice. While cookies are still warm, mound 1/2 teaspoon icing on each; icing will melt. Cool cookies completely.

Lemon Butter Cookies

Makes about 3 dozen

1/2 cup (1 stick) unsalted butter, room temperature
1/2 cup sugar
1 egg yolk
1/4 cup fresh lemon juice
1 1/2 teaspoons grated lemon peel
Pinch of salt

14 tablespoons sifted bleached all purpose flour
Powdered sugar

Preheat oven to 375°F. Grease baking sheets. Using electric mixer, cream butter and $^1/_2$ cup sugar until light and fluffy. Mix in yolk, then lemon juice, lemon peel and salt. Fold in flour. Drop batter by teaspoonfuls onto prepared sheets, spacing 2 inches apart. Bake until edges of cookies begin to brown, about 10 minutes. Cool slightly on baking sheets. Transfer to rack. Dust with powdered sugar and cool. Store in airtight container.

Pecan Butter Cookies

Makes about 2$^1/_2$ dozen

$^3/_4$ cup chopped pecans

$^1/_2$ cup all purpose flour
$^1/_2$ cup (1 stick) plus 1 tablespoon
    unsalted butter, room temperature

$^1/_3$ cup superfine sugar
1 egg yolk
$^1/_8$ teaspoon salt
28 to 32 pecan halves

Preheat oven to 375°F. Generously butter 2 baking sheets; set aside. Spread chopped pecans in single layer in pie plate and bake until lightly browned, about 10 minutes. Remove from oven (retain oven temperature) and let cool.

Finely grind nuts in processor or blender. Transfer to bowl. Add flour, butter, sugar, egg yolk and salt and mix with wooden spoon (or your hands) until well combined. Drop by rounded teaspoons onto prepared baking sheets, spacing well apart. Press a pecan half into each cookie. Bake until edges of cookies are golden brown, about 12 minutes. Let cool on baking sheet 3 minutes. Transfer to wire racks using wide spatula and let cool completely.

Sienese Almond Cookies (Ricciarelli di Siena)

Makes about 3 dozen

7 ounces almond paste
1 cup superfine sugar
2 egg whites, room temperature,
    beaten until foamy
1 teaspoon almond extract

1 teaspoon minced candied orange
    peel (optional)
Powdered sugar

Preheat oven to 275°F. Line baking sheets with parchment. Blend almond paste in processor until softened. Add superfine sugar and whites and mix until smooth. Blend in almond extract and orange peel. Drop batter by teaspoonfuls onto prepared sheets, spacing 1 inch apart. Bake until light brown and firm to touch, about 30 minutes. Cool on baking sheets. Sprinkle with powdered sugar.

Quick Macaroons

Make these cookies larger to use as a base for ice cream topped with strawberry sauce.
Or shape high rims on them to make cups for fruit filling.

Makes about 5$^1/_2$ dozen

4 egg whites
  Pinch of salt
$^3/_4$ cup sugar

1 teaspoon vanilla
2 cups shredded coconut

Preheat oven to 300°F. Lightly coat baking sheets with nonstick vegetable oil spray. Beat egg whites with salt until foamy. Gradually add sugar and vanilla, beating constantly until stiff but not dry. Stir in coconut. Drop batter onto prepared baking sheets by teaspoons. Bake until lightly browned, about 25 minutes. Store in airtight container.

Honey Bees

Makes 3 to 4 dozen

¹/₄ cup plus 2 tablespoons light honey
2 tablespoons (¹/₄ stick) unsalted butter
1 egg, beaten
³/₄ cup plus 2 tablespoons sifted whole wheat pastry flour

¹/₂ teaspoon cinnamon
¹/₄ teaspoon baking soda
¹/₈ teaspoon ground cloves
¹/₂ cup chopped raisins

Combine honey and butter in medium saucepan and warm over low heat until butter is melted. Let cool slightly.

Transfer honey mixture to large bowl of electric mixer. Add half of beaten egg and mix well. Sift flour, cinnamon, baking soda and cloves. Add to honey mixture and beat well. Stir in raisins.

Preheat oven to 400°F. Line baking sheet with waxed paper; oil paper. Drop dough by half-teaspoon (about ¹/₂-inch diameter) onto baking sheet. Bake 12 to 15 minutes. Cool on wire rack. Store in airtight container.

Ola's Sugar and Spice Cookies

These cookies freeze well.

Makes about 3¹/₂ dozen

1 cup sugar
³/₄ cup solid vegetable shortening
¹/₄ cup molasses
1 egg
2 cups all purpose flour

2 teaspoons baking soda
1 teaspoon cinnamon
³/₄ teaspoon ground ginger
³/₄ teaspoon ground cloves
¹/₄ teaspoon salt

Preheat oven to 375°F. Lightly grease baking sheets. Combine sugar, shortening, molasses and egg in large bowl and blend until smooth. Stir in remaining ingredients. Drop dough onto prepared sheets by teaspoons, spacing 2 inches apart. Bake until lightly browned, about 10 minutes (bake 2 more minutes for crisp cookie). Let cool on rack. Store in airtight container.

Benne Wafers

In the South Carolina low country, sesame seeds, called benne, are a good luck food, added to everything from cocktail snacks to cookies and candies.

Makes about 6 dozen

²/₃ cup sesame seed
¹/₂ cup (1 stick) butter, room temperature
¹/₂ cup sugar
¹/₂ cup firmly packed dark brown sugar

1 egg
1 cup sifted all purpose flour
1 teaspoon vanilla
¹/₈ teaspoon salt

Preheat oven to 275°F. Place sesame seed in pie plate and bake until lightly toasted, about 10 minutes. Let cool.

Preheat oven to 350°F. Lightly grease baking sheets. Cream butter with sugars in large bowl until light. Stir in egg. Add flour, vanilla, salt and sesame seed and mix well. Drop mixture by rounded half-teaspoon onto prepared sheets, spacing 3 inches apart.

Bake wafers until caramel colored, about 10 to 12 minutes. Remove from oven, let stand 1 minute and quickly transfer to wire racks. Let cool. Store in airtight containers.

Chinese Raisin-Oatmeal Cookies

Makes 4 dozen

²/₃ cup solid vegetable shortening, room temperature
1 cup firmly packed brown sugar
²/₃ cup sugar
2 eggs, beaten to blend
1 teaspoon vanilla
2 cups all purpose flour
1 cup rolled oats

1 teaspoon baking soda
1 teaspoon five-spice powder
¹/₂ teaspoon ground cloves
¹/₂ teaspoon cinnamon
1 cup raisins
1 cup chopped walnuts

Preheat oven to 350°F. Grease baking sheets. Cream shortening and both sugars in large bowl until light and fluffy. Mix in eggs and vanilla. Add flour, oatmeal, baking soda and spices and blend well. Stir in raisins and nuts. Drop batter onto baking sheets by heaping teaspoons. Bake until lightly browned, 10 to 12 minutes; do not overbake. Cool on racks.

Jumbo Oatmeal-Peanut Butter Cookies

Makes about 40

1 cup sugar
1 cup firmly packed light brown sugar
³/₄ cup (1¹/₂ sticks) margarine, room temperature
¹/₂ cup chunky peanut butter
2 eggs
¹/₄ cup milk

1 teaspoon vanilla
2 cups all purpose flour
1 teaspoon baking soda
1 teaspoon cinnamon
1 teaspoon salt
1¹/₂ cups quick-cooking oats
1 cup raisins

Preheat oven to 350°F. Grease baking sheets. Cream sugars with margarine and peanut butter in large bowl of electric mixer on medium speed. Add eggs 1 at a time, beating well after each addition. Beat in milk and vanilla. Mix in flour, baking soda, cinnamon and salt. Stir in oats and raisins. Drop dough onto prepared sheets by heaping tablespoons, spacing 2 inches apart. Bake until golden brown, about 15 minutes. Transfer to waxed paper and cool. Store in airtight container.

Peanut Drop Cookies

Makes 4 to 4¹/₂ dozen

¹/₂ cup (1 stick) unsalted butter, room temperature
1 cup firmly packed brown sugar
2 eggs
¹/₄ cup water
2 teaspoons finely grated lemon peel

2 cups unbleached all purpose flour
1 teaspoon baking powder
1¹/₄ cups whole salted roasted peanuts

Preheat oven to 350°F. Grease and flour baking sheets, shaking off excess. Cream butter in large bowl. Add sugar, blending well. Stir in eggs, water and lemon peel. Add flour and baking powder, mixing thoroughly. Stir in peanuts. Drop dough by teaspoon onto prepared baking sheets, spacing 1 inch apart. Bake until edges begin to brown, about 15 to 18 minutes. Transfer cookies to wire rack and let cool. Store in airtight container.

Peanut-Oatmeal Cookies

Makes about 3¹/₂ dozen

¹/₂ cup (1 stick) butter, room
  temperature
¹/₂ cup solid vegetable shortening
1 cup sugar
1 cup firmly packed dark brown
  sugar
2 eggs

1 teaspoon vanilla
2 cups all purpose flour
1 teaspoon baking soda
¹/₂ teaspoon baking powder
2 cups rice cereal, toasted in oven
2 cups quick-cooking oats
1 cup salted peanuts

Preheat oven to 350°F. Lightly grease baking sheets. Cream butter and shortening with sugars in large bowl. Add eggs 1 at a time, beating well after each addition. Beat in vanilla. Sift flour, baking soda and baking powder and add to butter mixture. Stir in cereal, oats and peanuts. Drop by heaping tablespoons onto prepared sheets, spacing 2¹/₂ inches apart. Bake until golden, 12 to 14 minutes. Store Peanut-Oatmeal Cookies in airtight container.

No-Bake Fudge Cookies

Makes about 4 dozen

2 cups sugar
¹/₂ cup milk
¹/₃ cup unsweetened cocoa powder
¹/₄ cup (¹/₂ stick) margarine, room
  temperature

¹/₄ cup peanut butter
3 cups quick-cooking oats

Combine sugar, milk, cocoa and margarine in medium saucepan. Place over medium-high heat and bring to boil, stirring constantly. Let boil 1 minute. Remove from heat. Mix in peanut butter. Add oats and blend thoroughly. Drop by teaspoon onto waxed paper. Let cool completely. Store cookies in airtight container.

Ranger Cookies

Makes about 4 dozen

1 cup solid vegetable shortening
1 cup granulated sugar
1 cup firmly packed brown sugar
2 eggs, room temperature
1 teaspoon vanilla
2 cups breakfast cereal
2 cups rolled oats

2 cups all purpose flour
2 teaspoons baking soda
1 teaspoon baking powder
¹/₂ teaspoon salt
1 cup coconut, or combination of
  coconut, chocolate chips, raisins
  and nuts

Preheat oven to 350°F. Lightly grease baking sheets. Cream shortening with sugars in large bowl. Add eggs one at a time, beating well after each addition. Stir in vanilla. Add cereal, oats, flour, baking soda, baking powder and salt. Fold in coconut. Drop dough by tablespoon onto prepared baking sheets, spacing 2 inches apart. Bake until golden, 14 to 16 minutes. Cool on rack. Store cookies in airtight container.

Date-Nut Goodies

Makes 2 to 2¹/₂ dozen

1 cup dates, chopped
1 cup pecans, chopped

1 cup sifted powdered sugar
1 egg white

Preheat oven to 350°F. Generously grease baking sheet. Combine dates, pecans and sugar in medium bowl. Add egg white, mixing well. Drop by teaspoon onto baking sheet. Bake until lightly browned, 12 minutes. Cool on wire rack. Store in airtight container.

Whole Wheat Walnut Nuggets

Makes 8 to 9 dozen

¹/₂ cup (1 stick) unsalted butter, room temperature
¹/₄ cup plus 2 tablespoons light honey
2 tablespoons molasses
1 egg, beaten
1¹/₄ cups sifted whole wheat pastry flour
1 teaspoon baking powder (without aluminum salts)

¹/₂ teaspoon cinnamon
¹/₂ teaspoon ground cloves
¹/₄ teaspoon baking soda
³/₄ cup rolled oats
¹/₄ cup plain yogurt
¹/₂ cup coarsely chopped walnuts
¹/₂ cup chopped raisins

8 dozen (about) walnut quarters (optional garnish)

Beat butter in large bowl of electric mixer until light and creamy. Add honey and molasses and beat again. Add egg and mix well. Sift flour, baking powder, cinnamon, cloves and baking soda into another bowl. Stir in rolled oats. Add dry ingredients to butter mixture alternately with yogurt, beating well after each addition. Stir in chopped walnuts and raisins and mix until just incorporated.

Preheat oven to 375°F. Line baking sheet with waxed paper; oil paper. Drop dough by teaspoon (about ¹/₂- to ³/₄-inch diameter) onto baking sheet. Press walnut quarter into top of each cookie, if desired. Bake 10 to 12 minutes. Cool on wire rack. Store in airtight container in cool, dark place.

Greek Walnut Cookies (Kourabiedes)

Makes about 2¹/₂ dozen

2¹/₄ cups unbleached all purpose flour
³/₄ cup walnuts
1 teaspoon baking powder
Pinch of salt
1 cup (2 sticks) unsalted butter, room temperature, cut into 4 pieces

2 tablespoons powdered sugar
1 egg yolk
2 teaspoons vanilla

¹/₂ to ³/₄ cup powdered sugar

Position rack in center of oven and preheat to 350°F.

Combine flour, walnuts, baking powder and salt in processor and mix until walnuts are finely ground. Transfer to small bowl and set aside. Add butter, 2 tablespoons powdered sugar, egg yolk and vanilla to work bowl and mix 1 minute, stopping machine once to scrape down sides of bowl. Return flour mixture to work bowl and mix using on/off turns just until flour is incorporated; do not overprocess (dough will be crumbly).

Drop dough onto baking sheet by tablespoons, rolling gently and then shaping into crescents. Bake until firm to touch, about 17 minutes; *do not brown.* Carefully transfer cookies to wire rack and let cool 10 minutes.

Sift remaining powdered sugar into small plastic bag. Place 1 cookie in bag and shake gently to coat all surfaces. Return cookie to rack and let cool. Repeat with remaining cookies. Store in airtight container.

Luscious Lunchbox Cookies

Makes about 7 1/2 dozen

2 cups unbleached all purpose flour
1 teaspoon baking soda
1 teaspoon cinnamon
1/2 teaspoon baking powder
1/2 teaspoon salt
1 cup (2 sticks) unsalted butter
1 cup sugar
1 cup firmly packed light brown sugar
2 eggs
1 teaspoon vanilla
1 cup quick-cooking oats
1 cup crisp rice cereal

Preheat oven to 350°F. Sift flour, soda, cinnamon, baking powder and salt into bowl. Cream butter with sugars in another large bowl until light and fluffy. Stir in eggs and vanilla. Gradually blend in flour mixture, beating until smooth. Fold in oats and rice cereal. Drop by tablespoon onto ungreased baking sheets. Bake cookies until golden, about 10 to 12 minutes. Cool on wire rack. Store in airtight container.

Glazed Apple Gems

Makes about 6 dozen

1/2 cup (1 stick) unsalted butter, room temperature
1 1/3 cups firmly packed brown sugar
1 egg
1 large apple, peeled, cored and finely chopped
1 cup raisins, finely chopped
1 cup walnuts or filberts, finely chopped
1/4 cup apple juice
1 teaspoon finely grated lemon peel
2 cups unbleached all purpose flour
1 teaspoon baking soda
1 teaspoon cinnamon
1 teaspoon freshly grated nutmeg

Glaze
1 1/2 cups sifted powdered sugar
3 tablespoons apple or lemon juice
1 tablespoon unsalted butter

Preheat oven to 375°F. Grease baking sheets. Cream butter with sugar in large bowl until light and fluffy. Stir in egg, apple, raisins, nuts, apple juice and lemon peel. Blend in flour, baking soda, cinnamon and nutmeg and mix well. Drop dough by tablespoon onto prepared sheets. Bake 10 to 12 minutes.

Meanwhile, prepare glaze. Blend sugar, juice and butter in processor or blender. Transfer mixture to bowl.

Remove cookies from oven. Let cool slightly on wire rack. Dip top of each warm cookie into glaze, swirling to cover. Return to wire rack (to allow excess glaze to drip through) and cool completely. Store in airtight container.

Caramel Crunch Cookies

Makes 40 cookies

7 $^7/_8$-ounce chocolate-covered toffee candy bars, broken into pieces
$^3/_4$ cup unbleached all purpose flour
$^3/_4$ cup rolled oats, regular or quick-cooking
$^1/_2$ teaspoon salt
$^1/_2$ teaspoon baking soda
6 tablespoons light brown sugar
6 tablespoons granulated sugar

2 teaspoons vanilla
1 egg
5 tablespoons unsalted butter ($^1/_2$ stick plus 1 tablespoon), room temperature
5 tablespoons solid vegetable shortening, room temperature

Position rack in center of oven and preheat to 375°F. Lightly grease 2 baking sheets and set aside.

Coarsely chop candy in processor using 6 on/off turns. Transfer to large bowl. Combine flour, oats, salt and baking soda in work bowl and mix 2 seconds. Add to candy. Blend sugars, vanilla and egg in work bowl 1 minute, stopping machine once to scrape down sides of bowl. Add butter and shortening and mix 1 minute. Return candy mixture to work bowl and blend briefly using on/off turns. (*Do not overmix; bits of candy should remain.*)

Drop batter onto baking sheets by teaspoonfuls, spacing 1 inch apart. Bake until golden, about 8 to 10 minutes. Let cool on wire rack. Transfer to airtight container and store in cool place.

Potato Chip Cookies

Makes about 14 dozen

2 cups (4 sticks) butter, room temperature
$3^1/_2$ cups all purpose flour
$1^1/_2$ cups sugar

2 teaspoons vanilla
3 ounces potato chips, crushed
Powdered sugar

Preheat oven to 350°F. Beat butter in medium bowl until light and fluffy. Gradually add flour, sugar and vanilla, mixing thoroughly. Blend in potato chips. Drop by teaspoon onto baking sheet. Bake until lightly golden, about 5 to 10 minutes. Let cool on baking sheet about 5 minutes. Sprinkle with powdered sugar. Transfer to wire rack and cool completely.

Chinese Noodle Cookies

Microwave these for a quick treat.

Makes about 4 dozen

1 12-ounce package peanut butter chips
1 5-ounce can chow mein noodles

$^1/_3$ cup chopped pecans
$^1/_3$ cup miniature marshmallows

Heat peanut butter chips in large glass bowl in microwave on High until melted, 2 to 4 minutes. Gently stir in noodles. Divide mixture into thirds. Stir pecans into 1 portion. Blend marshmallows into another (remainder is plain). Drop all 3 mixtures by rounded teaspoons onto waxed paper. Let cookies cool until set.

Pointers for Perfect Cookies

- Bring all ingredients to room temperature. Use only fresh flour, baking soda and baking powder. If flour has been stored in a humid place, it may have absorbed too much moisture, resulting in a cookie dough that is too soft. Check the expiration date for baking soda and baking powder. This is absolutely crucial for delicate cookie dough. All eggs (as called for in these recipes) should be large.

- Use shiny heavy aluminum baking sheets with low sides that won't deflect the heat. If only high-sided pans are available, turn them over and use the underside. Although large sheets can hold more cookies, pans should ideally be at least two inches smaller than the oven rack on all sides to allow heat to circulate freely.

- While the first batch of cookies bakes, shape, roll or cut uncooked dough as desired and arrange on lightly greased pieces of parchment paper or the shiny side of greased aluminum foil. Transfer paper to baking sheet. They will be all ready for the oven by the time the first batch is baked. Clean pan before reusing.

- For soft chewy cookies, allow less baking time; more for crisp ones.

- Recrisp cookies by baking in a 400°F oven for about three minutes.

- Glacéed fruit, pearl sugar, dipping chocolate and other quality baking supplies can often be purchased in quantity from a local baker or bakery supply.

- Use stiff cardboard to make cookie-cutter patterns or stencils through which powdered sugar can be sifted.

- To avoid excessive browning, use solid vegetable shortening as opposed to butter or oil to grease baking sheets or foil.

- If dough becomes too soft to handle, return it briefly to the refrigerator.

- If cookies are frosted or decorated, place a sheet of waxed paper between each layer before storing to prevent their sticking together.

- Package different cookies separately so they don't absorb other flavors.

Oatmeal-Molasses Lace Cookies with Lemon-Buttercream Filling

Makes about 30

Filling
- 2 teaspoons cornstarch
- 2 tablespoons fresh lemon juice
- 4 egg yolks, room temperature
- 1/4 cup sugar
- 10 tablespoons (1 1/4 sticks) unsalted butter, cut into 1/2-inch pieces, room temperature
- 1 teaspoon finely grated lemon peel

Cookie Dough
- Butter
- 3/4 cup sugar

- 3/4 cup packed quick-cooking oats
- 3/4 cup unbleached all purpose flour
- 1/2 teaspoon baking powder
- 10 tablespoons (1 1/4 sticks) unsalted butter, melted
- 1/4 cup milk
- 1/4 cup light molasses
- 1 teaspoon vanilla

For filling: Dissolve cornstarch in lemon juice. Whisk yolks, sugar, 4 tablespoons butter and lemon peel in heavy medium saucepan. Whisk in cornstarch. Whisk over low heat until smooth and thick enough to mound in spoon, about 5 minutes; *do not boil.* Cool to room temperature, whisking occasionally. Add remaining 6 tablespoons butter 1 piece at a time, whisking until smooth. Cover tightly and refrigerate until well chilled. (*Can be prepared 2 days ahead.*)

For cookies: Position rack in center of oven and preheat to 350°F. Dab butter in 3 places on rimless baking sheets or underside of overturned rimmed baking sheets. Line with foil, leaving 2-inch overhang on short ends. Combine sugar, oats, flour and baking powder in large bowl. Add melted butter, milk, molasses and vanilla and stir with fork until just blended. Let stand 15 minutes.

Drop batter onto prepared sheets by heaping teaspoonfuls, forming into 1-inch-diameter rounds and spacing 3 inches apart. Bake until cookies bubble and begin to brown around edges, 6 to 7 minutes. Transfer foil with cookies to work surface. Flatten cookies gently with spatula if necessary. Cool completely. (*Can be prepared 1 day ahead. Store in airtight container.*)

Just before serving, spread 3 teaspoons of filling evenly on bottom side of cookie, top with another cookie, bottom side in. Repeat procedure with remaining cookies and filling.

2 ❦ Hand-Shaped Cookies

This chapter is for those who prefer the "hands-on" approach—getting their hands into the cookie mixture. Whether you are pinching off bits of dough to be rolled into balls, forming long ropes to be twisted or cut, or rolling thick logs to be sliced or further shaped, you'll find making these cookies an extremely satisfying experience.

Perfect Sugar Cookies (page 19) are easy and delicious. Evoking memories of grandma's kitchen, Peanut Butter Favorites (page 31) start out as shaped balls, then are flattened on the cookie sheet with a fork to create the traditional crosshatch design. Slender ropes of dough are coated with sesame seed and then cut into 1¹/₂-inch lengths for flavorful Biscotti di Regina (page 21). Some recipes, such as Barcelona Almond Cookies (page 25) and Mandelbrodt with Chocolate Chips (page 29), require the dough be formed into a large loaf that is baked, then sliced and returned to the oven until it is crisp.

Ideal for make-ahead desserts and snacks, refrigerator cookies are a snap to prepare. Keep the plastic-wrapped logs of dough in the refrigerator (or freezer); then, when you want a freshly made treat, just slice them into rounds and bake. Try the classic Sugar Biscuits (page 36) or Mint-Fudge Cookies (page 38), which are mixed in the food processor for even greater ease. The most versatile recipe is the Christmas Butter Cookies (page 18). Although the recipe is included in this chapter, it has a number of variations and can also be simply dropped or rolled and cut into shapes. And don't let the name fool you—these are as delicious in the summer as they are in December.

Christmas Butter Cookies

Even cooking is the secret to success for all baked goods. If the last batch of cookies does not fill the baking sheet, invert a custard cup or small pan in any empty spaces to distribute the heat equally. If you suspect your oven has hot spots, turn the baking sheet around after five minutes in the oven.

Makes about 2¹/₂ dozen

¹/₂ cup (1 stick) unsalted butter, room temperature
¹/₂ cup sugar

2 egg yolks, room temperature
2 teaspoons vanilla
1 cup all purpose flour

Grease baking sheets. Cream butter with sugar in large bowl of electric mixer until fluffy. Beat in egg yolks and vanilla, stopping machine as necessary to scrape down sides of bowl. Add flour and continue beating just until mixed through; do not overbeat or cookies will be tough. Shape dough as desired (see below) and transfer to baking sheets. Chill before baking as needed.

Position rack in center of oven and preheat to 350°F. Bake cookies *one sheet at a time* until edges are brown and centers are just firm to touch, about 8 to 10 minutes. Cool on racks.

Variations

Drop butter cookies: Using 2 spoons (one to push the batter off the other), drop dough by spoonfuls onto prepared baking sheet, spacing cookies 2 inches apart. Smooth and round cookies using knife (or your finger) dipped in cold water. For firmer cookies that will not spread very much, refrigerate dough for 30 minutes before baking.

Pressed butter cookies: Turn dough out onto plate, cover with plastic wrap and refrigerate for 1 hour, or until dough is firm enough to mold. Fill cookie press with dough and press out onto prepared baking sheet, spacing 1 inch apart. Or spoon dough into damp pastry bag fitted with fluted tip (fill ²/₃ full) and pipe out onto prepared sheet, spacing 1 inch apart. In both instances, return dough to refrigerator if it becomes too soft to mold. Refrigerate cookies 30 minutes before baking.

Rolled butter cookies: Flatten dough into rectangle ¹/₂ inch thick on sheet of waxed paper. Cover with another sheet of waxed paper. Refrigerate for 45 minutes or until firm. Without removing paper, roll dough out into rectangle ¹/₄ inch thick. Return to refrigerator for 15 minutes. Discard top sheet of waxed paper. Using cookie cutter, knife or inverted beverage glass, cut as many shapes out of dough as possible. Arrange on prepared baking sheet, spacing 1 inch apart. Refrigerate 30 minutes. Meanwhile, gather scraps of dough into ball, reroll into rectangle, refrigerate and repeat rolling and cutting.

Refrigerator butter cookies: Turn dough out onto sheet of plastic wrap and, using plastic as aid, roll dough into cylinder 1 to 1¹/₂ inches thick. Wrap and refrigerate at least 12 hours. Slice into cookies ¹/₄ inch wide and transfer to prepared baking sheet. (Dough can be prepared ahead and refrigerated up to 1 week.) If desired, roll cylinder in pearl (coarse) sugar, cocoa, cinnamon or chopped nuts before slicing.

Filled butter cookies: To make a simple filled cookie, press thumb into formed cookie to make an indentation. Fill with jam, nuts, candy, chocolate chips, glacéed chestnuts or dried or glacéed fruit. Or put a very small amount of these ingredients (or almond paste) in center of dough rounds and fold in half, pressing edges together firmly. Fillings can also be sandwiched between 2 formed cookies or spread on refrigerator butter cookie dough rolled ¹/₄ inch thick. Roll dough as for jelly roll, refrigerate and slice into pinwheels.

Decorating cookies: Cookies can be decorated before or after baking. To decorate before, paint on a design with melted chocolate or a colored egg wash (egg yolk and water mixed with food coloring), or roll in cinnamon, cocoa or tinted sugar. Paint with milk, cream or a lightly beaten egg white and top with coconut, silver dragées, chocolate or colored sprinkles, sesame or poppy seed, chopped nuts, or dried or candied fruit.

To decorate cookies after they are baked, roll in cocoa or powdered sugar or brush with egg white and roll in cinnamon, tinted sugar or coconut. Or frost, cover with meringue and return briefly to a 500°F oven to brown. Cookies can also be glazed with powdered sugar that has been moistened with milk or cream. For a shiny surface, brush cookies lightly with warm corn syrup after baking.

Perfect Sugar Cookies

Makes 4¹/₂ to 5 dozen

2¹/₂ cups unbleached all purpose flour
1 teaspoon baking powder
1 teaspoon baking soda
Pinch of salt
1¹/₄ cups sugar

1 egg
2 teaspoons vanilla
1 cup (2 sticks) unsalted butter (room temperature), cut into tablespoon-size pieces

Position rack in center of oven and preheat to 325°F. Lightly grease baking sheets and set aside.

Combine flour, baking powder, baking soda and salt in processor and blend 2 seconds. Remove and set aside. Combine sugar, egg and vanilla in work bowl and blend 1 minute, stopping once to scrape down sides. Add butter and process 1 minute. Add dry ingredients and blend using on/off turns just until flour is incorporated; do not overprocess. Form into balls using about 2 teaspoons dough for each cookie. Arrange on prepared baking sheets, spacing 1¹/₂ inches apart. Bake until cookies are lightly browned, about 20 minutes. Let cool on racks. Store in airtight container.

Mexican Butter Cookies

Makes about 80

4¹/₂ cups all purpose flour
¹/₂ teaspoon baking powder
¹/₄ teaspoon salt
2 cups (4 sticks) butter, room temperature

2 cups chopped walnuts
1 teaspoon vanilla
1 cup powdered sugar

Preheat oven to 350°F. Sift flour, baking powder and salt into large bowl. Mix in butter until mixture forms soft dough. Add nuts and vanilla and mix well. Shape dough into walnut-sized balls. Arrange on baking sheet. Bake until set, about 15 minutes. Let cool slightly. Roll in powdered sugar. Store in airtight container.

Butterballs (Pallottole al Burro)

Makes about 3 dozen

¹/₂ cup (1 stick) butter, room temperature
¹/₄ cup sugar
2 tablespoons honey
1 cup plus 2 tablespoons all purpose flour

¹/₄ teaspoon (scant) baking soda
2 tablespoons dark rum
1¹/₄ cups coarsely ground walnuts or Brazil nuts

Powdered sugar

Cream butter, sugar and honey with electric mixer until smooth. Stir in flour and baking soda. Blend in rum, then nuts. Wrap dough in plastic and refrigerate until firm enough to handle, at least 1 hour, or overnight.

Preheat oven to 325°F. Lightly grease and flour baking sheets. Roll dough into 1-inch balls. Arrange on prepared sheets, spacing 1½ inches apart. Bake until firm and just beginning to color, 15 to 20 minutes. Cool slightly on racks. Roll in powdered sugar while still warm. Cool completely on racks. Store in airtight container.

Connie's Butter Cookies

For a nice variation, spread half the cookies with apricot, strawberry or blueberry preserves and top with another cookie.

Makes about 4 dozen

1 cup (2 sticks) butter, room temperature
7 tablespoons powdered sugar
1½ teaspoons vanilla

1½ cups plus 1 tablespoon all purpose flour
½ cup cornstarch
¼ to ½ cup powdered sugar

Position rack in center of oven and preheat to 325°F. Lightly grease baking sheets. Cream butter with 7 tablespoons powdered sugar. Mix in vanilla. Sift flour and cornstarch and blend into butter mixture. Shape into 1-inch balls. Transfer to prepared baking sheets, spacing 2 inches apart. Press each cookie lightly with bottom of floured glass. Bake until golden, 15 to 20 minutes. Cool 1 minute. Carefully remove from baking sheets. Cool completely. Store in airtight container. Sprinkle each cookie with powdered sugar before serving.

Black and White Cookies

Makes about 30

Cookies
1 cup (2 sticks) butter, room temperature
⅔ cup sugar
2 eggs, room temperature
2 teaspoons vanilla
½ teaspoon salt
2 cups all purpose flour

Icing
1¾ cups powdered sugar
4 tablespoons hot water
2 tablespoons vegetable oil
¼ teaspoon vanilla
¼ teaspoon fresh lemon juice
4 teaspoons unsweetened cocoa powder

For cookies: Preheat oven to 375°F. Lightly grease 2 baking sheets. Using electric mixer, cream butter with sugar in large bowl. Blend in eggs, vanilla and salt. Stir in flour using wooden spoon. Shape dough into 1¼-inch balls. Transfer to prepared sheets. Flatten tops slightly. Bake until lightly browned, 10 minutes. Cool on racks.

For icing: Blend 1 cup powdered sugar, 2 tablespoons hot water, 1 tablespoon oil, vanilla and lemon juice in small bowl until smooth. Blend remaining sugar, hot water and oil with cocoa powder in another small bowl until smooth. Spread half of bottom side of each cookie with white icing and half with dark. Let stand until icing is set. Store in airtight container.

Cream Cheese Cookies

Makes about 5 dozen

8 ounces cream cheese, room temperature
½ cup (1 stick) unsalted butter, room temperature
¾ cup sugar
1 to 2 tablespoons finely grated orange peel
1 teaspoon vanilla

1½ cups all purpose flour
2 teaspoons baking powder
Pinch of salt
½ cup chopped pecans

Powdered sugar

Combine cheese and butter in large bowl of electric mixer and cream at high speed until very light and fluffy. Gradually beat in sugar. Blend in grated orange peel and vanilla.

Sift flour, baking powder and salt together. Gradually add to cheese mixture at low speed. Stir in pecans. Form dough into ball. Wrap in waxed paper or plastic and chill 30 minutes.

Position rack in upper third of oven and preheat to 400°F. Grease 2 large baking sheets. Pinch off small walnut-size pieces of dough and roll into balls. Arrange on prepared baking sheets. Dip fork into powdered sugar and press into each cookie twice to form crosshatch design, flattening to ¼- to ⅜-inch thickness. Bake until cookies are just lightly browned and starting to set around edges, about 7 to 8 minutes (centers will be soft). Transfer to racks and cool completely before serving.

Biscotti di Regina (Queen's Cookies)

A very crisp cookie distinguished by the flavor of sesame seed.

Makes about 4½ dozen

1½ cups all purpose flour
⅔ cup sugar
¾ teaspoon baking powder
6 tablespoons (¾ stick) butter, melted

1 egg, beaten to blend
1½ teaspoons vanilla

¾ cup sesame seed

Preheat oven to 350°F. Combine flour, sugar and baking powder in medium bowl. Blend in butter, egg and vanilla with wooden spoon. Press dough together with hands.

Roll about ½ cup dough into ¾-inch-thick rope. Cut into 1½-inch lengths. Roll in sesame seed to coat completely. Arrange cookies on ungreased baking sheets, spacing ½ inch apart. Repeat with remaining dough. Bake until cookies are light golden, about 18 minutes. Cool completely on racks. Store cookies in airtight container.

For variation, add 2 teaspoons grated orange peel or ¾ teaspoon aniseed to dough.

Coconut Butter Cookies

Makes about 40

1 cup (2 sticks) unsalted butter, room temperature
$^1/_2$ cup sugar
$1^1/_2$ teaspoons vanilla
Pinch of salt

1 extra-large egg
$2^1/_2$ cups sifted all purpose flour
1 cup flaked coconut, lightly toasted
2 teaspoons grated lemon peel
Sugar

Position rack in upper third of oven and preheat to 350°F. Using electric mixer, cream butter until fluffy. Beat in $^1/_2$ cup sugar, vanilla and salt until light. Mix in egg. Gradually add flour and beat on low speed until smooth. Mix in coconut and peel. Form dough into $2 \times {}^3/_4$-inch crescents. Arrange $1^1/_2$ inches apart on ungreased baking sheets. Dip back of fork tines into sugar and press into top of cookies. Bake until light brown, 10 to 12 minutes. Let cool on wire racks. Store cookies in airtight container.

Butter Pecan Cookies

These would make a fine accompaniment to a pineapple-banana compote laced with Grand Marnier.

Makes about 5 dozen

2 cups pecans, toasted
$^1/_4$ cup sugar
1 cup (2 sticks) unsalted butter, cut into 8 pieces, room temperature
$1^1/_2$ teaspoons vanilla

$^1/_8$ teaspoon salt
2 cups unbleached all purpose flour

$^1/_2$ cup sugar
1 cup powdered sugar

Position rack in center of oven and then preheat to 300°F.

Chop pecans with $^1/_4$ cup sugar in processor until nuts are finely ground. Add butter, vanilla and salt and blend 1 minute, stopping once to scrape down work bowl. Add flour and process until just combined, using 2 or 3 on/off turns; do not overprocess.

Shape dough into $1^1/_4$-inch balls. Roll in $^1/_2$ cup sugar. Arrange on ungreased baking sheets, spacing 1 inch apart. Bake until just firm to touch, about 18 minutes. Transfer to rack and cool slightly. Dust warm cookies with powdered sugar. Cool completely before serving. (*Can be prepared ahead and refrigerated 5 days or frozen 4 months.*)

Nocciolette

Makes about $2^1/_2$ dozen

$^1/_2$ cup (1 stick) butter, room temperature
$^1/_3$ cup powdered sugar
1 cup all purpose flour
$^1/_2$ cup shelled hazelnuts, toasted, skinned and coarsely ground

$1^1/_2$ tablespoons honey

$^1/_2$ cup powdered sugar

Preheat oven to 350°F. Grease baking sheet. Cream butter with $^1/_3$ cup powdered sugar in large bowl until light and fluffy. Add flour, nuts and honey and beat until smooth.

Flour hands lightly. Form dough into $^1/_2$-inch balls. Transfer to prepared baking sheet, spacing 1 inch apart. Bake until firm, about 15 to 20 minutes. Transfer to rack and cool partially, then roll in remaining powdered sugar. Store in airtight container.

Italian Hazelnut Cookies (Biscottini di Nocciole)

This dough is ready in seconds.

Makes about 2¹/₂ dozen

³/₄ cup hazelnuts (4 ounces)
²/₃ cup sugar
2 egg yolks
1 teaspoon vanilla

¹/₂ teaspoon grated lemon peel
Pinch of salt

Sugar

Halve 15 hazelnuts, using sharp knife; set aside. Finely grind remaining nuts in processor. Blend in sugar thoroughly. With machine running, add yolks, vanilla, lemon peel and salt through feed tube and process until mixture forms ball, adding drops of water if necessary to make workable dough. Wrap dough in plastic or foil. Refrigerate 2 hours. (*Can be prepared 1 day ahead to this point.*)

Preheat oven to 350°F. Grease baking sheets. Form dough into ³/₄-inch balls. Arrange on prepared sheets, spacing 3 inches apart. Flatten to ¹/₈-inch thickness using bottom of glass dipped in sugar, twisting glass to prevent sticking. Firmly press hazelnut half, cut side down, into each cookie. Bake until cookies are dry and slightly golden, about 10 minutes. Immediately transfer cookies to racks. Cool completely. Store in airtight container.

Buttery Hazelnut Sticks

Chocolate and hazelnuts are often paired in German baked goods.

Makes about 4 dozen

¹/₂ cup (scant) hazelnuts (3 ounces)
¹/₂ cup (1 stick) unsalted butter, room temperature
¹/₃ cup plus 1 tablespoon sugar
1 medium egg
³/₄ teaspoon vanilla
1¹/₄ cups all purpose flour

Chocolate Glaze
1 egg white
¹/₃ cup sifted powdered sugar
¹/₂ teaspoon vanilla
1 ounce *each* unsweetened and semisweet chocolate, melted
2 tablespoons (about) warm water

Preheat oven to 325°F. Spread hazelnuts in shallow baking dish. Toast in oven 20 minutes, stirring occasionally. Cool 5 minutes. Rub hazelnuts back and forth between palms in small batches to loosen skins; discard skins. Transfer nuts to processor or blender and chop coarsely using on/off turns. Set aside 1¹/₂ tablespoons nuts for garnish. Grind remaining nuts finely.

Preheat oven to 350°F. Lightly grease baking sheets. Cream butter in medium bowl of electric mixer at medium speed. Gradually add sugar and beat until light and fluffy. Beat in egg and vanilla. Reduce mixer speed to medium-low and gradually blend in flour, beating until smooth. Fold in finely ground nuts. Spoon dough into pastry bag fitted with No. 4B (or similar) star tip. Pipe 1³/₄-inch-long strips of dough onto prepared baking sheets, spacing 1 inch apart. Bake until edges just begin to brown, about 9 to 11 minutes. Cool cookies several minutes, then transfer to wire racks to cool completely.

For glaze: Beat egg white in small bowl of electric mixer at medium-high speed until very frothy. Reduce speed to medium and gradually beat in powdered sugar and vanilla. Fold in melted chocolates. Stir in water a few drops at a time until mixture is glaze consistency.

Arrange cookies in even rows on rack with sides almost touching. Set rack over sheet of waxed paper. Using spoon, drizzle lines of glaze back and forth crosswise over cookies. Immediately sprinkle with reserved chopped hazelnuts. Let cookies stand until glaze is completely set. Store cookies in airtight container up to 1 week. (*Cookies can be frozen for up to 1 month.*)

Hazelnut Balls

Serve with brandied fruit and a cup of espresso for a light and elegant dessert.

Makes about 5 dozen

3/4 cup (1 1/2 sticks) unsalted butter, room temperature
2 cups sifted all purpose flour
1/4 cup sugar
1/4 cup grated bittersweet or semisweet chocolate
3 tablespoons Kahlúa or other coffee liqueur

1 teaspoon vanilla
1/2 teaspoon salt
1 1/2 cups finely ground lightly toasted and husked hazelnuts
1/2 cup coarsely ground lightly toasted and husked hazelnuts
Powdered sugar

Position rack in center of oven and preheat to 350°F. Lightly grease baking sheets. Using electric mixer, cream butter until light. Beat in flour, sugar, chocolate, Kahlúa, vanilla and salt. Mix in 1 1/2 cups finely ground hazelnuts. Shape dough into 1-inch balls. Roll in 1/2 cup coarsely ground nuts, coating thoroughly. Place on prepared sheet. Bake until golden brown, 25 to 30 minutes. Cool on rack. Dust with powdered sugar before serving. (*Can be stored in airtight container 1 week.*)

Hazelnut and Walnut Cookies

These flavorful cookies keep for months.

Makes about 5 dozen

3 cups unbleached all purpose flour
1 cup firmly packed dark brown sugar
1/2 cup sugar
2 teaspoons cinnamon
1 teaspoon baking powder
1/2 teaspoon salt

2 3/4 cups walnuts, coarsely chopped
3/4 cup hazelnuts, toasted (do not husk) and coarsely chopped
3 eggs, beaten to blend
1/3 cup vegetable oil

Preheat oven to 375°F. Grease 10 1/2 × 15 1/2-inch jelly roll pan. Sift first 6 ingredients into large bowl. Mix in all nuts. Reserve 2 tablespoons egg for glaze. Add remaining egg and oil to flour and mix until crumbly dough forms. Pat into prepared pan. Brush with reserved egg. Bake until beginning to color, about 15 minutes. Remove from oven; reduce temperature to 300°F. Cut cookies into diamonds 1 1/2 inches long on each side. Place on baking sheets. Bake until cookies begin to dry, about 15 minutes. Transfer to rack and cool completely. Store in airtight container.

Walnut Cookies

These delicate, shortbread-style cookies are perfect with ice cream.

Makes 40

2 cups all purpose flour
2/3 cup ground walnuts
1 cup (2 sticks) unsalted butter, room temperature
1/2 cup powdered sugar

Powdered sugar

Combine flour and walnuts in small bowl. Cream butter with 1/2 cup sugar in bowl of electric mixer until fluffy. Blend in flour mixture 1/2 cup at a time until firm dough forms. Cover with plastic and refrigerate 30 minutes.

Preheat oven to 350°F. Grease baking sheets. Divide dough into 10 pieces. Knead 1 piece briefly in palm until smooth and slightly softened. Form into ball.

Place on prepared sheet and flatten to 4-inch round. Decorate edges by pressing with back of fork tines. Pierce all over with fork. Cut into 4 wedges; do not separate. Repeat with remaining dough. Bake until medium brown, about 20 minutes. Recut cookies to separate. Place on racks. Sift powdered sugar over. Cool completely. Store in airtight container.

Almond Jumbles

Makes about 4 dozen

11 tablespoons unsalted butter, room temperature
1/2 cup sugar
1 egg
1 teaspoon grated lemon peel
11/4 cups all purpose flour

1 teaspoon baking powder
1/4 teaspoon salt
1/2 cup pulverized blanched almonds (21/4 ounces)

Using electric mixer, cream butter with sugar until light and fluffy. Add egg and lemon peel and beat until fluffy. Combine flour, baking powder and salt. Gently blend into butter mixture. Add almonds and mix. Wrap in plastic and refrigerate 45 minutes.

Preheat oven to 350°F. Line baking sheets with parchment. Cut dough into 4 pieces. Return 3 pieces to refrigerator. Roll 1 piece into 1/2-inch-thick rope. Cut into 2-inch lengths. Roll each end between palm and floured surface to taper. Form into S shapes. Transfer to prepared sheets, spacing 2 inches apart. Repeat with remaining dough. Bake cookies until light golden brown, about 10 minutes. Cool on racks. Store in airtight container.

Barcelona Almond Cookies (Carquinyolis)

An exceptionally crunchy cookie.

Makes about 51/2 dozen

21/3 cups all purpose flour
1 cup plus 1 tablespoon sugar
1 teaspoon baking soda
1/2 teaspoon salt
2 eggs

2 tablespoons grated lemon peel
1/4 teaspoon almond extract
1/2 pound whole blanched almonds

Preheat oven to 350°F. Butter baking sheet. Combine flour, sugar, baking soda, salt, eggs, lemon peel and almond extract in processor and mix well. Blend in almonds by hand (dough will be sticky). Divide dough in half. Transfer half to baking sheet. Pat and shape into 11/4-inch-wide and 3/4-inch-high rectangular loaf with slightly rounded top. Repeat with remaining dough. Bake until lightly golden, about 22 to 25 minutes. Immediately cut crosswise into 3/4-inch-wide slices. Increase oven temperature to 450°F. Arrange cookies cut side down on baking sheet. Bake until just golden, about 3 to 4 minutes, watching carefully and turning once if necessary. Cool on rack before serving.

Fave Dolci (Sweet Beans)

Chewy cookies from southern Italy that are served on All Souls' Day. The custom stems from the ancient tradition of offering beans to Pluto and Proserpina, god and goddess of the underworld in Roman mythology.

Makes about 5 dozen

1 cup unblanched almonds
1 cup sugar
1/3 cup unsalted butter, cut into 1/2-inch pieces
1 egg
2 teaspoons grated lemon peel

1 teaspoon orange flower water
1/2 teaspoon cinnamon
1/2 cup plus 2 tablespoons all purpose flour

Grind almonds finely in processor using on/off turns. Add sugar and blend until powdery. Add butter, egg, lemon peel, orange flower water and cinnamon and process to paste. Mix in flour until just incorporated, using several on/off turns (dough will be sticky). Transfer to medium bowl. Cover with plastic. Refrigerate overnight.

Preheat oven to 350°F. Grease and flour baking sheets. Roll rounded teaspoons of dough into short thick cylinders. Arrange on prepared sheets, spacing 2 inches apart. Using finger or handle of wooden spoon, press indentation in side of each to form into lima bean shape. Flatten slightly with hands. Bake until cookies are just beginning to color, about 16 minutes. Cool on baking sheets 5 minutes; transfer to racks and cool completely. Store in airtight container.

Sweet Pistachio Cookies

Makes 36

1 cup solid vegetable shortening, room temperature
1 cup powdered sugar, sifted
2 cups all purpose flour

36 pistachios, shelled

Using electric mixer, cream shortening and sugar in medium bowl until light, about 2 minutes. Sift flour onto shortening and mix until dough is smooth. Cover dough with plastic and refrigerate for 20 minutes.

Preheat oven to 350°F. Roll dough into 36 walnut-size pieces. Transfer to baking sheets. Press one pistachio into top of each. Bake until bottoms are light brown, 20 to 25 minutes. Cool cookies slightly on wire rack. Serve warm, or cool completely and then store in airtight container.

Date-Pecan Balls

Makes about 55

1 cup (2 sticks) butter, room temperature
1/2 cup sugar
2 teaspoons vanilla
2 cups all purpose flour

2 cups pecans, finely chopped
1 cup pitted dates, chopped

Powdered sugar

Cream butter with sugar in large bowl. Mix in vanilla. Stir in flour. Add pecans and dates and mix thoroughly. Shape dough into walnut-size balls. Transfer to waxed paper-lined tray. Freeze 15 minutes or refrigerate overnight.

Preheat oven to 350°F. Grease baking sheets. Arrange cookies on prepared pans, spacing 1 inch apart. Bake until golden, about 15 to 20 minutes. Roll in powdered sugar. Let cool slightly. Roll in powdered sugar again. Store cookies in airtight container.

First Dates

Makes about 3 dozen

1 cup sugar
2 eggs
1/2 cup unbleached all purpose flour
1/2 teaspoon baking powder
1/4 teaspoon salt

1 cup whole dates, pitted and chopped
1 cup pecans or walnuts, chopped
1/4 cup sugar

Preheat oven to 350°F. Generously grease 8-inch glass baking dish. Beat 1 cup sugar and eggs in large bowl until fluffy. Sift flour, baking powder and salt into sugar mixture and blend well. Fold in dates and nuts. Turn into prepared pan. Bake *exactly* 30 minutes. Remove from oven *immediately* and stir, mixing well. Cool completely. Shape into bite-size balls. Roll in remaining sugar. Store in airtight container.

Fruit Basket Cookies

Makes about 4 dozen

12 whole candied cherries (about 1/4 cup)
4 ounces pitted dates
2 ounces dried apricots
1/4 cup golden raisins
1 1/2 cups sifted all purpose flour

1/2 cup (1 stick) butter, room temperature
3/4 cup firmly packed brown sugar
1 egg

1 tablespoon fresh orange juice
1/2 teaspoon lemon extract
1/2 teaspoon baking soda
1/2 teaspoon cream of tartar
1/4 teaspoon salt
1/2 cup finely chopped pecans
1/4 cup finely chopped walnuts

Preheat oven to 350°F. Grease baking sheets. Combine cherries, dates, apricots and raisins in small bowl. Transfer half of mixture to processor. Add 1 tablespoon flour and chop finely using on/off turns. Turn into bowl. Repeat with remaining fruit.

Cream butter with sugar in large bowl. Beat in egg. Stir in orange juice and lemon extract. Sift baking soda, cream of tartar, salt and remaining flour over egg mixture and blend well. Stir in chopped fruit and nuts. Chill dough slightly. Shape into 1-inch balls. Transfer to prepared sheet and press gently with fork to flatten. Bake until golden, about 18 to 20 minutes. Cool on wire rack. Store cookies in airtight container.

Brutti ma Buoni (Ugly but Good)

From Florence, these are a combination of fruit and nuts that are really not ugly, just somewhat irregularly shaped.

Makes about 3 dozen

1 1/2 cups blanched almonds (8 ounces)
1 1/3 cups powdered sugar
1/4 teaspoon vanilla
1/4 teaspoon almond extract
Pinch of salt

1 egg white
1/3 cup coarsely chopped walnuts
3 tablespoons minced moist dried apricots

Preheat oven to 350°F. Grease and flour baking sheet. Grind almonds in processor until finely powdered and beginning to hold together, stopping occasionally to scrape down sides of work bowl, about 3 minutes. Blend in sugar, vanilla, almond extract and salt. With machine running, pour egg white through feed tube and blend until mixture forms ball. Transfer to medium bowl.

Knead in walnuts and apricots. Form dough into 1-inch balls. Pinch into irregular shapes. Arrange on prepared sheet, spacing 1 inch apart. Bake until just beginning to brown, 13 to 15 minutes. Cool on racks. Store in airtight container.

Pat's Biscotti

These are delicious with espresso.

Makes about 6 dozen

2 cups sugar
2 cups coarsely chopped walnuts
1 cup (2 sticks) butter, melted
1/4 cup aniseed
1/4 cup anisette
2 tablespoons water

2 teaspoons vanilla
6 eggs, room temperature
5 1/2 cups all purpose flour
1 tablespoon baking powder

Mix sugar, nuts, butter, aniseed, anisette, water and vanilla in large bowl. Beat in eggs 1 at a time. Combine flour and baking powder and stir into mixture. Cover with plastic wrap and refrigerate 3 hours.

Preheat oven to 375°F. Grease baking sheets. Divide dough into 5 pieces. Shape each into long loaf 1/2 inch high and 2 inches wide on prepared sheets, spacing 4 inches apart. Bake until firm to touch, about 20 minutes. Let cool 30 minutes. Maintain oven temperature at 375°F.

Cut loaves diagonally into 1/2- to 3/4-inch-thick slices. Arrange slices cut side down on sheets. Bake until light brown, about 7 minutes on each side. Cool completely on racks. Store in airtight container.

Anisebrodt

Makes about 6 dozen

1 cup sugar
3/4 cup plus 2 tablespoons vegetable oil
4 eggs
2 tablespoons water
2 tablespoons poppy seed

4 teaspoons baking powder
1 teaspoon vanilla
1 teaspoon anise extract
4 1/2 cups all purpose flour

Preheat oven to 325°F. Grease baking sheets. Combine first 8 ingredients in large bowl and beat well. Stir in flour and knead until dough is no longer sticky, about 10 minutes. Shape dough into 5 strips about 2 inches wide, 14 inches long and 1/3 inch high. Arrange on baking sheets. Bake until golden, about 20 minutes. Cut strips diagonally into 1-inch-wide bars. Return to oven and bake 5 minutes. Turn cookies on side and bake another 5 minutes. Let cool on rack. Store in airtight container.

Mandelbrodt with Chocolate Chips

Mandelbrodt freezes well.

Makes about 3 dozen

3 cups all purpose flour
2 teaspoons baking powder
1/2 teaspoon salt
1 cup plus 1 tablespoon vegetable oil
1 cup sugar
3 eggs

1 cup finely chopped pecans
4 ounces semisweet chocolate chips

5 tablespoons sugar
1 tablespoon cinnamon

Preheat oven to 375°F. Grease 2 baking sheets. Mix flour, baking powder and salt in medium bowl. Beat oil, 1 cup sugar and eggs in large bowl. Gradually add 2 cups flour mixture, beating constantly. Fold in pecans and chocolate chips. Add remaining flour and mix well.

Lightly flour hands. Divide dough into fourths. Transfer to baking sheets. Shape into flat loaves about 3 inches wide and about 3/4 inch high. Combine remaining sugar and cinnamon in small bowl and sprinkle evenly over each. Bake 20 minutes. Cut each loaf into 1/2-inch slices. Turn slices cut side up and continue baking until toasted and golden, about 15 minutes. Cool completely. Store in airtight container.

Cornish Fairings

Makes about 2 dozen

1 1/2 cups plus 2 tablespoons all purpose flour
2 teaspoons baking soda
2 teaspoons baking powder
1 teaspoon cinnamon
1 teaspoon freshly grated nutmeg
1/2 teaspoon ground cloves
1/2 teaspoon allspice

1/2 teaspoon ground ginger
1/2 cup (1 stick) unsalted butter, cut into pieces, room temperature
1 teaspoon grated orange peel
1/2 cup sugar
1/3 cup English golden syrup*
1 cup coarsely chopped unskinned almonds

Sift together flour, soda, baking powder, cinnamon, nutmeg, cloves, allspice and ginger. Transfer to processor. Add butter and orange peel and blend using on/off turns until mixture resembles coarse meal. Mix in sugar. Add syrup and 1/2 cup chopped almonds and mix using on/off turns until dough just gathers into ball.

Preheat oven to 400°F. Line 2 baking sheets with parchment paper. Place remaining 1/2 cup almonds in small bowl. Working quickly to prevent over-softening, roll dough into walnut-size balls. Press one side of each ball into almonds, flattening slightly. Arrange on prepared baking sheet nut side up, spacing evenly. Bake until golden brown, 9 to 10 minutes. Cool 4 to 5 minutes. Transfer to rack using spatula. Cool completely before serving. Store in airtight container.

*Available in specialty food stores. Light molasses can be substituted and will give the cookies a more robust flavor.

Parkin Cookies

A parkin is a traditional English oatmeal and ginger cake from Yorkshire. It is always eaten on Guy Fawkes Day, November 5. These cookies are great any time of year.

Makes about 4¹/₂ dozen

2³/₄ cups oatmeal
1¹/₂ cups plus 2 tablespoons all purpose flour
¹/₂ cup plus 2 tablespoons sugar
1¹/₂ teaspoons baking powder
1 teaspoon cinnamon
1 teaspoon ground ginger
1 teaspoon allspice

¹/₂ cup (1 stick) butter, cut into pieces
³/₄ cup Lyle's Golden Syrup*
1 egg, beaten
54 almond halves (about 2 ounces)

Preheat oven to 325°F. Grease baking sheets. Combine oatmeal, flour, sugar, baking powder, cinnamon, ginger and allspice in large bowl and mix well. Cut in butter. Stir in syrup and egg and mix well. Form dough into 1-inch balls. Transfer to prepared baking sheets. Lightly press almond half into each ball. Bake until browned, about 15 minutes. Cool on rack.

*Available in specialty foods stores. Light molasses can be substituted.

Swedish Snowballs

Makes 3¹/₂ to 4 dozen

1 cup (2 sticks) unsalted butter cut into 4 pieces, room temperature
³/₄ cup firmly packed dark brown sugar
1 egg yolk
1 teaspoon vanilla

³/₄ teaspoon ground cardamom
¹/₈ teaspoon salt
2 cups unbleached all purpose flour

1¹/₄ cups powdered sugar

Position rack in center of oven and then preheat to 350°F.

Blend butter, brown sugar, yolk, vanilla, cardamom and salt in processor until fluffy, stopping as necessary to scrape down sides of work bowl, about 1 minute. Add flour in circle atop mixture and blend just until incorporated using 2 to 3 on/off turns; do not overprocess dough mixture.

Shape dough into balls, using 2 teaspoons of mixture for each. Arrange on baking sheets, spacing 2 inches apart. Bake until cookies are set but not brown, about 12 minutes. Transfer to rack and cool 10 minutes.

Pour powdered sugar into paper bag. Add several cookies; close bag and shake gently to coat with sugar. Return cookies to rack. Repeat with remaining cookies. Cool completely. (*Can be prepared 4 days ahead and kept at room temperature or 3 months ahead and frozen. Store in airtight container.*)

Cardamom Cookies

These flavorful tea biscuits are best the same day they are baked.

Makes about 40

¹/₂ cup sugar
6 tablespoons (³/₄ stick) butter, room temperature
1 egg
1¹/₂ cups plus 2 tablespoons unbleached all purpose flour

1¹/₂ teaspoons freshly ground cardamom seed
³/₄ teaspoon baking powder
2 tablespoons sugar
¹/₂ teaspoon cinnamon

Position rack in center of oven and preheat to 375°F. Grease large baking sheet. Using electric mixer, cream ¹/₂ cup sugar, butter and egg until light and fluffy. Sift flour, cardamom and baking powder; mix into butter until just blended.

Divide dough into 4 pieces. Roll each on lightly floured surface to 14-inch-long rope. Arrange on prepared sheet, spacing 2 inches apart. Flatten each to 1/4 inch, using spatula. Mix 2 tablespoons sugar with cinnamon; sprinkle over ropes. Bake until slightly puffed, beginning to color and dry to touch, 10 to 12 minutes. Remove from oven and cut diagonally into 1 1/4-inch-wide pieces. Cool completely on rack. Store in airtight container.

Peanut Butter Favorites

Makes 5 dozen

3/4 cup peanut butter (preferably homemade)*
1/2 cup (1 stick) unsalted butter, room temperature
1 1/4 cups unbleached all purpose flour
1/2 cup sugar

1/2 cup firmly packed brown sugar
1 egg
1 teaspoon baking soda
1/4 teaspoon baking powder
Pinch of salt

Preheat oven to 350°F. Lightly grease baking sheets. Combine peanut butter and butter in large bowl. Add flour, sugars, egg, baking soda, baking powder and salt and mix well. Roll dough into 1-inch balls and arrange 3 inches apart on baking sheets. Press crisscross pattern on cookies using fork. Bake until golden, about 10 to 12 minutes. Transfer to wire rack and let cool. Store in airtight container.

*Natural foods stores carry peanut butter with no added oil or salt that can be substituted for homemade peanut butter.

No-Flour Peanut Butter Cookies

For an unusual morning treat, serve these cookies hot for breakfast.

Makes about 30 cookies

1 cup peanut butter
1 cup sugar

1 egg

Preheat oven to 350°F. Lightly grease baking sheet. Combine all ingredients in medium bowl and blend well. Form dough into 1-inch balls. Arrange on prepared sheet. Bake until lightly browned, about 10 to 12 minutes. Cool on rack. Store in airtight container.

Peanut and Almond Butter Cookies

Makes 4 dozen

1 cup sugar
1 cup firmly packed brown sugar
1 cup (2 sticks) margarine, room temperature
2 eggs, room temperature, beaten to blend
1/2 cup chunky peanut butter
1/2 cup almond butter,* well blended

1 teaspoon almond extract
2 1/2 cups all purpose flour
1 1/2 teaspoons baking soda
1 teaspoon baking powder
1/2 teaspoon salt

Sugar

Blend 1 cup sugar, brown sugar, margarine, eggs, peanut and almond butters and extract in large bowl. Sift together flour, baking soda, baking powder and salt. Add to butter mixture and blend well. Refrigerate at least 1 hour or overnight.

Preheat oven to 375°F. Lightly grease baking sheets. Roll dough into walnut-size balls. Transfer to baking sheets, spacing 2 to 3 inches apart. Flatten each slightly with fork dipped in sugar, making crisscross pattern. Bake until golden brown, 10 to 12 minutes; do not overbake. Cool on racks.

*Almond butter is available at natural foods stores.

No-Bake Chocolate Mini Balls

Makes 6 1/2 dozen

1 1/4 cups milk
1 1/4 cups sugar
3 tablespoons unsweetened cocoa powder
3/4 cup (1 1/2 sticks) margarine, room temperature
1 tablespoon instant coffee powder

1 teaspoon sweet red wine
1/4 teaspoon rum flavoring
4 cups crushed butter cookies

2 cups shredded coconut or coarsely chopped unsalted peanuts

Combine milk, sugar and cocoa in 2-quart saucepan. Cook over low heat, stirring constantly, until sugar dissolves, about 10 minutes. Remove from heat. Add margarine, coffee powder, wine and rum flavoring and stir until margarine melts. Add cookie crumbs and mix thoroughly. Cover tightly and refrigerate overnight.

Form dough into 1-inch balls. Roll in coconut or peanuts, covering completely. Place in small fluted paper cups. Cover and chill until ready to serve.

Chimneysweeps

Rich and chewy chocolate macaroons.

Makes about 30

1 cup blanched almonds
2/3 cup sugar
2 egg whites
3 ounces imported bittersweet (not unsweetened) or semisweet chocolate, melted and cooled slightly

1/4 cup blanched almonds, toasted and chopped
1 tablespoon unsweetened cocoa powder (preferably Dutch process)
30 whole blanched almonds

Position rack in center of oven and preheat to 325°F. Line baking sheets with parchment; butter lightly. Finely grind 1 cup almonds with 2 tablespoons sugar in processor. Add 1 white and blend 10 seconds. Add half of remaining sugar and blend 10 seconds. Repeat with remaining white and sugar. Transfer to medium bowl. Mix in melted chocolate, chopped almonds and cocoa powder. Drop batter by tablespoons onto prepared sheet, spacing 1 1/2 inches apart. Using moistened fingers, shape dough into 3/4-inch-high 1 1/4-inch-diameter mounds. Set whole almonds in center of each, pointed end up. Bake until cookies are dry and just firm on outside but soft in center, about 12 to 15 minutes. Cool on rack. Store in airtight container.

Foothill House Sweet Dreams

Makes about 6 dozen

1 cup (2 sticks) unsalted butter
1½ cups firmly packed light brown sugar
1 egg, room temperature
1 teaspoon vanilla
2 cups unbleached all purpose flour
1 teaspoon baking soda
1 teaspoon cinnamon

1 teaspoon ground ginger
½ teaspoon salt
1 12-ounce package semisweet chocolate chips
1 cup chopped walnuts

1 cup powdered sugar

Cream butter using electric mixer. Beat in brown sugar, egg and vanilla. Combine flour, baking soda, cinnamon, ginger and salt. Blend into butter mixture. Fold in chocolate chips and walnuts. Refrigerate until firm. (*Can be prepared 1 day ahead.*)

Preheat oven to 375°F. Lightly grease baking sheets. Break off small pieces of dough; roll between palms into 1-inch rounds. Dredge rounds in powdered sugar. Arrange rounds on prepared sheets, spacing at least 2 inches apart. Bake 10 minutes. Let cool 5 minutes on sheets. Transfer to racks and cool. Store in airtight container.

Cocoa Cookies

Make the dough ahead of time and refrigerate, microwaving these delectable treats only as you need them. The dough can be wrapped tightly and refrigerated for up to three days.

Makes about 30 cookies

¾ cup (1½ sticks) unsalted butter, room temperature
¾ cup sugar
1 egg
1¾ cups all purpose flour
¼ cup unsweetened cocoa powder
1 teaspoon baking powder

½ teaspoon salt
1 teaspoon vanilla
½ cup chopped walnuts
Sugar

Combine butter, ¾ cup sugar and egg in processor or electric mixer and blend until light and fluffy. Sift together flour, cocoa, baking powder and salt. Blend into butter mixture, beating well. Stir in vanilla and nuts. Divide dough and roll into 1-inch balls. Roll evenly in sugar. Transfer to platter. Cover and refrigerate until ready to cook.

Space balls of dough 1½ inches apart on paper plate. Flatten tops slightly with spoon. Cook uncovered on High until cookies are puffed, about 1 minute for 2 cookies; 1¼ minutes for 4 cookies; 2 minutes for 8 cookies; and 3 minutes for 12 cookies (for crisper cookies, let cook an additional few seconds). Let cool slightly before removing from plate (they will firm as they stand). Transfer to rack and cool completely.

❦ *Filled Cookies*

Hussars' Biscuits

Makes about 3¹/₂ dozen

1 cup (2 sticks) unsalted butter,
room temperature
²/₃ cup (scant) sugar
2 egg yolks
¹/₂ teaspoon vanilla
2¹/₂ cups all purpose flour

¹/₄ cup (about) red currant jelly
¹/₄ cup (about) black currant jelly
6 tablespoons (about) finely slivered
almonds

Preheat oven to 400°F. Lightly grease baking sheets. Cream butter in medium bowl of electric mixer at medium speed. Add sugar and beat until light and fluffy. Blend in yolks and vanilla. Gradually mix in flour to form dough.

Pinch off walnut-size pieces of dough and roll into balls. Arrange on prepared baking sheets, spacing 1¹/₂ inches apart. Press deep indentation in center of each ball with thumb. Bake cookies 8 minutes. Remove from oven and fill indentations with about ¹/₂ teaspoon jelly, using red currant for half of cookies and black currant for remainder. Continue baking until jelly is slightly melted and edges of cookies just begin to brown, about 5 minutes. Cool 2 to 3 minutes, then transfer to racks. Arrange several almond slivers atop jelly to resemble wheel spokes. Cool cookies completely. Store cookies in single layer in airtight container for up to 3 weeks; do not freeze.

Thumbprint Poppy Seed Cookies

Makes about 3¹/₂ dozen

1 cup (2 sticks) butter, room
temperature
¹/₂ cup sugar
2 egg yolks
1 teaspoon vanilla

2 cups all purpose flour
3 tablespoons poppy seed
¹/₈ teaspoon salt

Strawberry jelly

Using electric mixer, cream butter with sugar in large bowl. Add yolks and vanilla and beat until light and fluffy, about 3 minutes. Add flour, poppy seed and salt and blend well. Cover and chill overnight.

Preheat oven to 375°F. Form dough into 1-inch balls. Arrange on ungreased baking sheets, spacing about 2 inches apart. Let soften several minutes at room temperature. Make indentation in center of each using thumb. Bake cookies until lightly browned, 12 to 15 minutes. Transfer to racks. While still warm, press centers again with thumb. Just before serving, fill centers with jelly.

Jammies

*Makes 4¹/₂ to 5 dozen
cookies*

³/₄ cup (1¹/₂ sticks) butter, room
temperature
²/₃ cup sugar
1 egg
1 teaspoon vanilla

2 cups all purpose flour
¹/₂ teaspoon baking powder
¹/₂ teaspoon cinnamon
Jam

Preheat oven to 350°F. Cream butter with sugar in large bowl. Add egg and vanilla and beat well. Combine flour, baking powder and cinnamon and add gradually to creamed mixture, blending well after each addition. Divide into four equal portions, rolling each into cylinder about 12 inches long. Transfer to baking sheet(s). Make an indentation about 1/4 inch deep down center of each cylinder and fill with jam. Bake until golden, about 15 minutes. Let cool slightly, then slice cylinders diagonally into cookies 3/4 inch wide.

Chocolate-filled Thumbprint Cookies

Makes about 3 dozen

1 cup (2 sticks) butter, room temperature
1 cup firmly packed light brown sugar
2 teaspoons vanilla
3 cups sifted all purpose flour
1/2 cup (scant) semisweet chocolate chips
5 teaspoons milk
1/2 teaspoon salt
1/2 cup powdered sugar

Chocolate Filling
1 3/4 cups semisweet chocolate chips
2 tablespoons solid vegetable shortening
1/4 cup light corn syrup
2 tablespoons water
1 teaspoon vanilla

Preheat oven to 350°F. Blend butter, brown sugar and vanilla in large bowl until creamy. Stir in flour, chocolate chips, milk and salt and mix well. Form dough into 1-inch balls. Arrange on ungreased baking sheets. Indent center of each ball by pressing firmly with thumb. Bake cookies until golden, about 12 to 15 minutes. Immediately roll in powdered sugar, covering completely. Arrange on rack and let cool 15 minutes.

Meanwhile, prepare filling: Melt chocolate and shortening in top of double boiler over hot (but not boiling) water. Remove from over water. Stir in remaining ingredients until smooth. Let cool 5 minutes.

Place generous 1/2 teaspoon chocolate filling in each thumbprint. Store cookies in airtight container.

Raspberry-Coconut Drops

Makes about 4 dozen

1/4 cup firmly packed light brown sugar
Peel of 1 medium lemon
1/2 cup (1 stick) unsalted butter (room temperature), cut into 4 pieces
1 egg, separated

1 teaspoon cinnamon
1/8 teaspoon ground cloves
Pinch of salt
1 cup unbleached all purpose flour
1 cup shredded coconut
1/2 cup raspberry preserves

Combine sugar and lemon peel in processor and mix until finely minced. Add butter, egg yolk, cinnamon, cloves and salt and blend 1 minute, stopping machine once to scrape down sides of bowl. Add flour and mix using on/off turns just until flour is incorporated; do not overprocess. Shape dough into ball. Wrap in plastic and seal tightly. Refrigerate until firm, at least 30 minutes.

Position rack in center of oven and preheat to 300°F. Lightly grease 2 baking sheets. Beat egg white in small bowl until foamy. Spread coconut evenly in shallow dish. Roll dough into teaspoon-size balls. Dip into egg white, coating entire surface. Roll evenly in coconut. Arrange drops on baking sheet, spacing 1½ inches apart. Make indentation in centers by pressing gently with thumb. Bake until coconut is lightly browned, about 17 minutes. Transfer cookies to wire rack and let cool (if necessary, press centers while drops are still hot). Stir preserves until smooth. Spoon into center of each drop. Store in airtight container. (*Unfilled Raspberry-Coconut Drops can be frozen. Thaw before filling.*)

❦ Refrigerator Cookies

Sugar Biscuits

Makes about 5 dozen

2½ cups all purpose flour
1 teaspoon baking powder
¼ teaspoon salt
   Pinch of freshly grated nutmeg
½ cup (1 stick) unsalted butter, room temperature

¾ cup plus 2 tablespoons sugar
2 tablespoons milk
1 egg
1 teaspoon vanilla

2 tablespoons sugar

Sift together flour, baking powder, salt and nutmeg. Cream butter with sugar in large bowl of electric mixer. Stir in milk, egg and vanilla. Blend in flour mixture. Roll dough into 1½- to 2-inch cylinder. Wrap in waxed paper or parchment paper. Chill until very firm. (*Can be prepared 1 day ahead.*)

   Preheat oven to 375°F. Cut cylinder into ⅛-inch-thick slices. Transfer slices to ungreased baking sheet, spacing about 2 inches apart. Press fork tines into edges of slices to decorate (dipping fork in cold water if necessary to prevent sticking). Sprinkle centers of slices with remaining 2 tablespoons sugar. Bake until edges just begin to color, 8 to 10 minutes. Let biscuits cool on wire rack before serving.

Crystal Butter Cookies

Makes about 5 dozen

¾ cup (1½ sticks) butter, room temperature
½ cup (scant) sugar
½ teaspoon vanilla
1¾ cups all purpose flour
   Pinch of salt

1 egg yolk
2 cups broken rock candy

Line baking sheets with parchment paper. Beat together butter, sugar and vanilla on low speed. Add flour and salt all at once and continue beating until well blended, about 2 minutes. Wrap dough and refrigerate 30 minutes.

   Preheat oven to 400°F. Divide dough into 3 equal portions. Roll each into cylinder about 1¼ inches in diameter. Refrigerate for 15 minutes.

   Beat egg yolk. Roll cylinders in yolk and then into candy, pressing lightly so candy adheres to dough. Cut into slices ½ inch thick. Bake until set and lightly golden, about 12 minutes.

Gingersnaps

Makes about 30 dozen

1½ cups firmly packed light brown
    sugar
¼ cup blackstrap or dark molasses
1 egg, room temperature
1 cup (2 sticks) butter, melted and
    slightly cooled
2⅔ cups sifted all purpose flour

2 teaspoons ground ginger
1½ teaspoons ground cloves
1½ teaspoons cinnamon
1½ teaspoons baking soda
⅜ teaspoon salt

Granulated sugar

Combine brown sugar, molasses and egg in large bowl and mix well. Beat in butter. Stir in flour, ginger, cloves, cinnamon, baking soda and salt. Turn dough out onto lightly floured surface and shape into 4 long logs. Roll logs back and forth several times. Cut each in half crosswise. Shape logs to diameter of about ⅝ inch. Freeze until thoroughly chilled, about 1 hour.

    Preheat oven to 350°F. Lightly grease baking sheet (preferably nonstick). Pour sugar into pie plate to depth of about ¼ inch. Remove 1 log from freezer and cut into ¼-inch slices. Dip slices into sugar, turning several times to coat entire surface and pressing dough to spread and flatten to thickness of about ⅛ inch. Transfer slices to prepared sheet, spacing about 1 inch apart. Bake until lightly browned but still soft, about 6 to 8 minutes. Let cool until almost hard, about 30 seconds. Using spatula, quickly transfer cookies to sheet of waxed paper; *if cooled too long, cookies will cling to pan and break when removed.* (If cookies harden before removal from baking sheet, return to oven for about 30 seconds.) Sprinkle with sugar. Repeat with remaining dough. (*Cookies can be prepared 1 month ahead. Store in airtight container.*)

Ginger Coin Cookies

Minced crystallized ginger gives these refrigerator cookies their unusual flavor. The dough can be made well ahead and frozen. Let thaw slightly before slicing into cookie rounds.

Makes about 5 dozen

1 cup (2 sticks) unsalted butter,
    room temperature
1 cup powdered sugar, sifted
2½ cups sifted all purpose flour
3 tablespoons finely minced
    crystallized ginger

1 teaspoon ground ginger
¼ teaspoon salt

Cream butter with powdered sugar in large bowl. Add all remaining ingredients and blend well. Form dough into cylinder about 1¾ inches in diameter. Wrap in plastic and refrigerate until firm enough to slice, at least 2 hours, or freeze about 45 minutes.

    Preheat oven to 400°F. Cut dough into ¼-inch-thick slices. Arrange slices on ungreased baking sheets. Bake until lightly browned, about 8 minutes. Transfer cookies to wire racks to cool. Store in airtight container. (*Cookies can be prepared ahead, wrapped tightly in foil and frozen.*)

Espresso Nut Cookies

Makes about 3 dozen

2 cups all purpose flour
1 teaspoon baking powder
1/8 teaspoon salt
1/2 cup (1 stick) butter, room temperature
1 cup sugar
1 egg

1 tablespoon instant espresso powder dissolved in 1 tablespoon hot water and cooled
1/2 cup finely chopped walnuts

Sift flour, baking powder and salt. Cream butter in large bowl. Gradually add sugar, beating until fluffy. Add egg and cooled espresso and beat well. Blend in flour mixture; stir in nuts. Divide dough in half and shape into 2-inch cylinders. Wrap in waxed paper and chill (or wrap in foil and freeze).

When ready to bake, preheat oven to 375°F. Grease baking sheets. Slice cylinders into 1/4-inch rounds and arrange on prepared sheets. Bake until firm and lightly browned, about 8 to 10 minutes. Transfer cookies to racks and let cool. Store in airtight container.

Mint-Fudge Cookies

Makes about 3 dozen

1 cup minus 2 tablespoons unbleached all purpose flour
1/2 teaspoon baking soda
1/4 teaspoon salt
3 ounces sweet cooking chocolate, cut into 1-inch pieces
2 ounces unsweetened chocolate, cut into 1-inch pieces
1/2 cup sugar
1/2 cup firmly packed light brown sugar

1 tablespoon unsweetened cocoa powder
1/2 cup (1 stick) unsalted butter (room temperature), cut into 4 pieces
1 egg
1 teaspoon vanilla extract
3/4 teaspoon peppermint extract

Combine flour, baking soda and salt in processor and mix 2 seconds. Transfer to small bowl and set aside. Add chocolates, sugars and cocoa powder to work bowl and chop, using 5 on/off turns, then mix until chocolate is very fine, about 1 minute. Add butter, egg and extracts and mix 1 minute, stopping machine once to scrape down sides of bowl. Return flour mixture to work bowl and blend using on/off turns just until flour is incorporated; do not overprocess.

Divide dough into 4 equal portions. Arrange each on sheet of plastic wrap. Using plastic as aid, shape dough into 2 × 4-inch cylinders. Seal and refrigerate until firm, 1 hour. (*Can be prepared ahead to this point and frozen.*)

Position rack in center of oven and preheat to 375°F. Cut dough into 1/2-inch slices. Arrange on baking sheet, spacing 2 inches apart. Bake until edges are lightly browned, about 8 minutes. Let cool 3 to 4 minutes. Transfer to wire rack and cool completely. Store in airtight container.

3 ❧ Rolled Cookies

Pull out the rolling pin, bring out the cookie cutters, and call in the children—or the child in you—and share the fun: You're sure to enjoy the collection of rolled cookies in this chapter.

Your imagination and creativity have full scope with these favorites. The method is easy: Chill the dough until firm, roll it out nice and thin, and cut the dough into shapes with cookie cutters (a drinking glass, small tartlet mold or sharp knife will also work). Some cookies are decorated before or after baking, some others are frosted or dusted with powdered sugar just before serving.

Grandma's Cakies (page 40) are simple, sugar-topped cookies that are sure to please young and old. Papassinos (page 43), loaded with fruit, almonds and walnuts, are traditionally made into diamonds or squares. Of course, we could not leave out Gingerbread Cookies (page 47), a heartwarming treat in any collection.

Adding a small amount of jam filling to a rolled cookie is a great way to dress up this simple pastry. Some of our best of this type come from Europe: Half-Moon Cookies (page 51), filled with strawberry preserves, is a special Swedish treat. Poilâne's Sablé Cookies (page 52), come from a famous bakery in Paris. Little Rascals (page 52), a Swiss specialty, have three tiny holes revealing the brightly colored filling of red raspberry jam.

Although the recipes in this chapter will indicate what shape of cutter to use, don't let that restrict you. Use your imagination to create your own fanciful shapes.

Grandma's Cakies

Adults enjoy these simple sweets with coffee; children love them with milk.

Makes about 25

1 teaspoon baking soda
½ cup sour cream, room temperature

¾ cup (1½ sticks) butter
1½ cups sugar
3 eggs, beaten to blend
1½ teaspoons vanilla

¼ teaspoon salt
4 cups (or more) all purpose flour

½ cup all purpose flour
¼ cup sugar
Additional sugar

Stir baking soda into sour cream. Let stand until puffy, 5 to 10 minutes.

Using electric mixer, beat butter until light and fluffy. Gradually beat in 1½ cups sugar and eggs. Blend in sour cream mixture, vanilla and salt. Stir in 4 cups flour 1 cup at a time, adding up to 2 tablespoons more flour if dough appears sticky. Wrap and chill 3 hours.

Preheat oven to 375°F. Lightly grease baking sheets. Divide dough into thirds. Wrap and refrigerate 2 pieces. Mix ½ cup flour and ¼ cup sugar. Sprinkle work surface with some of flour mixture. Roll 1 piece of dough out to thickness of ¼ inch, working quickly to prevent stickiness. Cut out rounds using 3-inch cutter. Gather scraps and refrigerate. Reroll and cut additional rounds. Arrange 7 rounds on prepared sheet. Sprinkle tops with sugar. Repeat with remaining dough. Bake until lightly golden on bottom, about 10 minutes; tops should not brown at all. Cool completely before serving. (*Can be prepared 3 days ahead and stored in airtight container or several weeks ahead and frozen.*)

Gertrud's Lemon-Glazed Stars

Makes 6 dozen

1 cup (2 sticks) unsalted butter, cut into tablespoons, slightly chilled
¾ cup sugar
1 tablespoon finely grated lemon peel
1½ teaspoons cinnamon
¼ teaspoon salt
2 egg yolks

1⅓ cups finely ground unblanched almonds
1⅓ cups finely ground walnuts
2 cups all purpose flour

2 cups sifted powdered sugar
¼ cup fresh lemon juice

Cream butter, sugar, lemon peel, cinnamon and salt in large bowl of electric mixer until light and fluffy. Beat in yolks. Mix in almonds and walnuts, then stir in flour. Shape dough into flat round. Wrap in foil. Refrigerate until firm enough to roll, 2 to 3 hours.

Lightly grease baking sheets. Divide dough into 4 pieces; return 3 to refrigerator to prevent drying. Roll remainder out on generously floured pastry cloth or between 2 sheets of waxed paper to thickness of 3/16 inch. Cut out cookies using floured 2½- to 3-inch star cutter. Arrange on prepared baking sheets, spacing about 1 inch apart. Repeat with remaining dough. Gather scraps and refrigerate 30 minutes. Reroll and cut additional stars.

Position rack in center of oven and preheat to 375°F. Bake cookies until lightly browned, about 8 minutes. Remove from sheets with wide spatula and let cool on racks.

Beat powdered sugar into lemon juice in bowl until smooth. Dip tops of cookies into glaze. Turn cookies upright, letting excess glaze drip back into bowl. Let cookies dry 1 hour. Store in foil- or waxed paper-lined airtight container in cool dry place.

Lemon Tea Biscuits

These are great with a cup of Earl Grey tea.

Makes about 5 dozen

1²/₃ cups self-rising flour*
³/₄ cup (1¹/₂ sticks) well-chilled unsalted butter, cut into small pieces

1 cup powdered sugar
1 teaspoon grated lemon peel
1 egg, beaten to blend

Place flour in medium bowl. Rub in butter until fine crumbs form. Add sugar and lemon peel. Add egg and mix gently just until stiff dough forms. Gather into ball; flatten into disc. Wrap in plastic; chill 30 minutes.

Preheat oven to 350°F. Line baking sheets with parchment. Roll dough out on lightly floured surface to thickness of ¹/₈ inch. Cut into 2-inch rounds, using fluted cookie cutter. Transfer to prepared sheets. Gather scraps, roll out and cut additional cookies. Bake until edges are light brown, 10 to 12 minutes. Cool on racks. Store in airtight container.

*If self-rising flour is unavailable, 1²/₃ cups all purpose flour mixed with ¹/₂ teaspoon baking powder, ¹/₂ teaspoon baking soda and ¹/₄ teaspoon salt can be used.

Lemon Hearts

Makes about 2 dozen

Lemon-Almond Cookies
1¹/₄ cups whole blanched almonds
3 4 × ³/₄-inch strips lemon peel, halved
¹/₂ cup plus 3 tablespoons sugar
3 egg yolks
¹/₂ teaspoon almond extract

Lemon Glaze
1 cup powdered sugar
2 tablespoons fresh lemon juice
1 tablespoon water

For cookies: Preheat oven to 350°F. Line baking sheet with parchment. Grind almonds to fine powder in processor. Set aside. Finely mince lemon peel with sugar in processor, 1 to 2 minutes. Add yolks and almond extract and process until mixture is thick and light in color, about 1 minute. Add ground almonds. Blend until ball forms.

Roll dough out between sheets of waxed paper to thickness of ¹/₄ inch. (If pastry becomes too soft to work, freeze 10 to 15 minutes.) Remove top sheet of paper. Cut out cookies using 2- to 2¹/₂-inch heart-shaped cutter, dipping cutter in water between each one. Transfer to prepared sheet. Reroll scraps and cut additional cookies. Bake until just beginning to color, 9 to 11 minutes. Transfer cookies and parchment to racks and cool completely. (*Cookies can be prepared 2 weeks ahead and stored in airtight container.*)

For glaze: Combine all ingredients in small bowl and mix until smooth.

Dip top of each cookie into glaze. Wipe off excess with knife. Dry on rack set over waxed paper.

Almond Cookies

Makes about 6 dozen

3/4 cup (1 1/2 sticks) butter, room
temperature
6 tablespoons sugar
1/2 teaspoon almond extract
2 cups all purpose flour
1/8 teaspoon salt

1 egg white, beaten to blend (glaze)
1/3 cup minced blanched almonds
1/8 teaspoon cinnamon

Cream butter with 4 tablespoons sugar and almond extract until light and fluffy. Sift together flour and salt. Beat into butter mixture. Gather dough into ball; flatten into disc. Wrap in plastic and refrigerate 1 hour.

Preheat oven to 350°F. Roll dough out on lightly floured surface to thickness of 1/8 inch. Using fluted pastry wheel, cut dough into 1 × 2-inch strips. Arrange on ungreased baking sheets. Brush with glaze. Combine remaining 2 tablespoons sugar, almonds and cinnamon. Sprinkle over strips. Bake until golden brown around edges, about 10 minutes. Cool cookies on racks.

Cashew Cookies

Makes about 3 dozen

2 cups sifted cake flour
1/2 teaspoon baking powder
1 cup (2 sticks) butter, room
temperature

1/2 cup powdered sugar
1 cup chopped, roasted and salted
cashews

Sift flour with baking powder. Cream butter and sugar in large bowl until smooth. Stir in flour mixture and cashews. Refrigerate dough about 1 hour.

Preheat oven to 375°F. Remove half of dough from refrigerator. Roll out on lightly floured surface to thickness of 1/4 inch. Cut into 2-inch squares. Arrange on ungreased baking sheets. Repeat with remaining dough. Bake until golden brown, about 10 minutes. Cool on rack. Store cookies in airtight container.

Hazelnut Biscuits with Coffee Butter Frosting

Buttery, delicate and pretty cookies to serve with tea or coffee.

Makes about 24

Biscuits
2/3 cup hazelnuts (3 ounces), toasted
and husked
1/4 cup (1/2 stick) unsalted butter,
room temperature
2 tablespoons sugar
1/2 cup all purpose flour

Frosting
1/2 cup powdered sugar

2 tablespoons (1/4 stick) unsalted
butter, room temperature
2 teaspoons instant coffee powder
2 teaspoons hot water

Chopped toasted hazelnuts

For biscuits: Pulverize hazelnuts in processor. Using electric mixer, cream butter with sugar. Gently mix in hazelnuts and flour. Gather dough into ball; flatten into disc. Wrap in plastic and refrigerate 30 minutes.

Preheat oven to 325°F. Line baking sheets with parchment. Roll dough out between sheets of plastic wrap to thickness of 1/8 inch, refrigerating briefly if too soft to roll. Cut into 2-inch rounds. Arrange cookies on prepared sheets, spacing

1½ inches apart. Gather scraps, roll out and cut additional cookies. Bake until beginning to color, 10 to 15 minutes. Cool 5 minutes on sheets. Transfer to rack and cool. (*Can be prepared 5 days ahead. Store in airtight container.*)

For frosting: Using electric mixer, cream sugar and butter until light and fluffy. Dissolve coffee in hot water. Blend into butter mixture.

Spoon frosting into pastry bag fitted with small plain tip. Pipe dot of frosting in center of each cookie. Sprinkle with chopped hazelnuts and serve.

Sardinian Raisin and Nut Cookies (Papassinos)

Shortbread-type cookies loaded with fruit, almonds and walnuts and delicately flavored with Marsala.

Makes about 3½ dozen

½ cup (1 stick) unsalted butter, room temperature
¾ cup sugar
2 teaspoons grated orange peel
2 eggs
2 tablespoons Marsala, Sherry or fresh orange juice
1½ cups all purpose flour
¼ teaspoon salt

⅔ cup raisins
⅔ cup coarsely chopped toasted almonds
⅔ cup coarsely chopped walnuts
⅓ cup powdered sugar, sifted
1 scant tablespoon fresh orange juice

Cream butter, ¾ cup sugar and orange peel using electric mixer. Beat in eggs 1 at a time. Blend in Marsala. Stir in flour and salt, then raisins and nuts. Wrap dough in plastic. Refrigerate at least 4 hours or overnight.

Preheat oven to 350°F. Roll dough out on well-floured surface to thickness of ⅜ inch. Cut into 1½-inch diamonds or squares using floured knife. Arrange on ungreased baking sheets, spacing 1 inch apart. Bake until light golden, about 23 minutes. Transfer to racks. Mix powdered sugar with orange juice. Brush glaze over warm cookies. Cool to room temperature. Store in airtight container.

Grandma's Shortbread

Makes 2 dozen

2 cups all purpose flour
½ cup powdered sugar
⅓ cup rice flour
½ teaspoon salt

1 cup (2 sticks) unsalted butter, room temperature

Sift flour, powdered sugar, rice flour and salt. Place butter in large bowl. Sift flour mixture over butter. Mix until butter and flour are completely incorporated. Transfer dough to lightly floured surface and knead until very soft, about 5 minutes. Roll dough into cylinder. Cover tightly with plastic wrap and refrigerate 1 hour.

Preheat oven to 350°F. Knead dough on lightly floured surface 2 minutes. Roll dough out to rectangle ¼ inch thick. Cut into 24 circles using 2-inch cookie cutter or glass. Transfer to baking sheets. Bake cookies until lightly golden around edges, about 20 minutes. Cool on racks.

Macadamia Shortbread Hearts

8 servings

3/4 cup macadamia nuts

1¼ cups sifted all purpose flour
6 tablespoons sugar
1 teaspoon grated lemon peel
¼ teaspoon salt

½ cup (1 stick) well-chilled unsalted
butter, cut into ½-inch pieces
2 tablespoons beaten egg

½ teaspoon vanilla

Preheat oven to 325°F. Rinse salt off macadamia nuts; pat dry. Spread on baking sheet and toast until golden brown, 10 to 15 minutes. Cool. Cut macadamia nuts into ¼-inch pieces.

Blend flour, sugar, lemon peel and salt in processor. Add butter and process until coarse meal forms, using on/off turns. Add egg and vanilla and process until just blended. Transfer to bowl. Gently mix in nuts. Form dough into ½-inch-thick rectangle. Cover with plastic and refrigerate at least 2 hours. (*Can be prepared 1 day ahead.*)

Position rack in lower third of oven and preheat to 325°F. Lightly butter baking sheet. Let dough soften at room temperature 10 minutes. Roll out between sheets of plastic to thickness of ¼ inch. Cut into 2½- to 3-inch hearts, using heart-shaped cookie cutter. Transfer to prepared sheet. Gather scraps, reroll and cut additional cookies. Refrigerate cookies 15 minutes. Bake until golden brown, about 18 minutes. Cool on rack. (*Shortbread hearts can be prepared 1 day ahead.*)

Shortbread Brittany Style (Palets Bretons)

Makes about 80

1¼ cups (2½ sticks) butter, room
temperature
1 teaspoon ground cardamom
1 teaspoon orange flower water
1 cup sugar
2½ cups sifted all purpose flour

¼ cup cornstarch
Pinch of salt

1 egg yolk
3 tablespoons whipping cream

Cream butter in large bowl of electric mixer. Beat in cardamom and orange flower water. Stir in sugar, using rubber spatula, just until incorporated. Combine flour, cornstarch and salt. Fold into butter mixture until ball forms. Set dough on 14 × 16-inch piece of plastic wrap. Cover with second piece of plastic wrap. Roll dough out ¼ inch thick. Refrigerate 1 hour.

Preheat oven to 375°F. Cut chilled dough into cookies using 1½-inch round cutter (return scraps to refrigerator to firm). Arrange cookies on heavy baking sheets, spacing 1½ inches apart. Blend yolk and cream. Brush thinly on each cookie. Trace crisscross pattern on top of each, using fork tines. Bake until golden brown, about 7 minutes. Transfer to wire rack and cool completely. Repeat rolling, cutting and baking with chilled scraps. Store cookies in airtight container.

Lemon Sablés

Makes 4 dozen 2-inch cookies

Pâte Sablée
- ²/₃ cup almond meal
- ²/₃ cup sifted powdered sugar
- 11 tablespoons unsalted butter, room temperature
- 1 egg
- 2 teaspoons finely grated lemon peel
- pinch of salt
- 1¹/₂ cups plus 2 tablespoons pastry flour or all purpose flour

Lemon Glaze
- 2 tablespoons sifted powdered sugar
- 1 egg yolk
- 1 tablespoon fresh lemon juice

For dough: Mix almond meal and powdered sugar in processor to fine powder, about 10 seconds. Transfer to bowl of electric mixer. Add butter and beat until light. Blend in egg, lemon peel and salt. Beat in flour all at once until just combined; do not overmix. Gather dough into ball. Wrap in plastic and refrigerate at least 3 hours.

Divide dough in half. Wrap half in plastic and return to refrigerator to prevent drying. Roll remainder out on generously floured surface to thickness of ³/₁₆ inch. (Keep surface and rolling pin well floured to prevent sticking.) Cut out rounds using floured 2-inch scalloped cutter. Gather scraps and reroll additional rounds. Set on baking sheets. Refrigerate 30 minutes.

For glaze: Blend powdered sugar, egg yolk and lemon juice.

Preheat oven to 350°F. Lightly brush top of each round with glaze. Score design atop each with fork tines. Bake until lightly browned around edges, about 15 minutes. Cool completely on rack. Store in airtight container.

Honey Lebkuchen Hearts

Makes about 8 dozen 2- to 3¹/₂-inch cookies

- ³/₄ cup honey
- ¹/₂ cup sugar
- 2 ounces unsweetened chocolate, coarsely chopped

- 3 cups plus 2 tablespoons all purpose flour
- 1 tablespoon cinnamon
- 1¹/₄ teaspoons mace
- ¹/₂ teaspoon ground cloves
- ¹/₄ teaspoon allspice
- ¹/₄ teaspoon (scant) ground cardamom
- ¹/₄ teaspoon baking powder
- ¹/₄ teaspoon baking soda
- ³/₄ cup slivered almonds, finely ground (3 ounces)

- 3 tablespoons minced candied lemon peel
- Grated peel of ¹/₂ medium lemon

- 1 medium egg
- 1¹/₂ teaspoons vanilla

Icing
- 1 cup sifted powdered sugar
- 1 tablespoon fresh lemon juice
- 1¹/₂ to 2 teaspoons (about) water
- Cinnamon red-hot candies and silver sprinkles
- 1 to 2 drops red food coloring (optional)

Blend honey and sugar in heavy small saucepan. Stir in chocolate. Place over very low heat, stirring occasionally, until sugar dissolves and chocolate is melted, about 15 to 20 minutes; do not boil. Remove from heat and let cool.

Sift flour, spices, baking powder and baking soda; set aside. Blend finely ground almonds with candied and grated lemon peels in small bowl.

Beat egg in medium bowl of electric mixer at medium speed until light and fluffy. Gradually beat in cooled honey mixture and vanilla. Reduce mixer speed to low and blend in almond mixture. Gradually beat in dry ingredients, stirring in last 1/2 cup by hand if mixer begins to slow down (dough will be slightly soft and sticky). Divide dough in half; wrap in plastic and flatten into disc. Refrigerate at least 6 hours, preferably overnight.

Preheat oven to 350°F. Generously grease baking sheets. Dust work surface and rolling pin generously with flour. Working quickly so dough stays chilled, roll dough out slightly less than 1/4 inch thick, lifting frequently and dusting with flour as necessary to prevent sticking. (Dough can also be rolled out between sheets of plastic wrap or waxed paper.) Using heart-shaped cutters of various sizes, cut out cookies one at a time; brush off any excess flour. Immediately arrange on prepared baking sheets, spacing 3/4 inch apart (if some hearts are much larger than others, bake in different batches). If dough and trimmings become too sticky to handle, rechill and reroll. Bake until cookies are almost firm and very lightly browned at edges, about 10 to 12 minutes; do not overbake. Let cool 1 to 2 minutes, then transfer to racks to cool completely.

For icing: Mix powdered sugar, lemon juice and 1 1/4 teaspoons water in small bowl until smooth. Stir in additional water a few drops at a time until icing holds its shape but is soft enough to be piped through pastry bag fitted with No. 2 (fine-line) decorator tip. Pipe attractive edging around each heart, making dots, straight or wavy lines, crisscross or scallops. Pipe additional icing onto each heart and top with cinnamon candies and silver sprinkles. (If desired, prepare extra half recipe of icing and tint with food coloring. Pipe onto cookies for further decoration.) Let cookies stand until icing is completely set. Store cookies in airtight containers for up to 4 weeks. (*Cookies can be frozen up to 2 months.*)

Belgrade Bread

These small spice cookies are rolled and cut to resemble bread.

Makes about 3 dozen

1 cup (scant) all purpose flour
Scant 1/8 teaspoon *each* cinnamon, ground cloves and allspice
1/4 cup (about 3/4 ounce) coarsely ground walnuts
1/4 cup minced candied lemon peel
1 tablespoon minced candied orange peel
1 medium egg
1/3 cup plus 1 tablespoon sugar
1 tablespoon fresh lemon juice
Grated peel of 1 small lemon
1 to 2 tablespoons all purpose flour

Icing
1/2 cup sifted powdered sugar
1 tablespoon dark rum
1 1/2 teaspoons (about) fresh lemon juice
2 tablespoons (about) finely chopped mixed candied orange peel, lemon peel and/or cherries

Sift 1 scant cup flour with spices; set aside. Toss ground walnuts with candied peels in small bowl. Beat egg in medium bowl of electric mixer at medium speed until very frothy, 2 minutes. Gradually add sugar, lemon juice and grated lemon peel, beating until light. Reduce mixer speed to low and gradually beat in sifted dry ingredients. Fold in walnut mixture. Blend in remaining 1 to 2 tablespoons flour 1/2 tablespoon at a time until dough forms ball but is still soft and slightly moist. Wrap in plastic and flatten into disc. Refrigerate dough for at least 6 hours, preferably overnight.

Preheat oven to 350°F. Dust work surface and rolling pin generously with flour. Working quickly so dough stays chilled, roll dough into rectangle slightly less than 1/4 inch thick, lifting frequently and dusting with flour as necessary to prevent sticking. Using pastry wheel or sharp knife, cut dough lengthwise into 1 1/4-inch-wide strips, flouring wheel if necessary. Cut strips crosswise into 2-inch lengths. Immediately arrange on ungreased baking sheets, spacing 1/2 inch apart. Bake cookies until edges just begin to brown, about 10 to 12 minutes. Let stand 2 minutes, then transfer cookies to wire racks to cool slightly.

For icing: Mix powdered sugar, rum and 3/4 teaspoon lemon juice in small bowl until smooth. Stir in additional lemon juice a few drops at a time until icing is easily spreadable. Using knife, spread icing lightly over warm cookies. Immediately press 2 or 3 bits of candied orange or lemon peel or cherries firmly into icing. Let stand on racks until icing is completely set. Store cookies in airtight container for up to 4 weeks. (*Cookies can be frozen for several months.*)

Gingerbread Cookies

Makes about 10 dozen

2 cups unbleached all purpose flour
1 cup cake flour
2 teaspoons ground ginger
1 1/2 teaspoons cinnamon
1 teaspoon baking powder
3/4 teaspoon salt
1/2 teaspoon baking soda
1/2 teaspoon freshly grated nutmeg
1/2 teaspoon ground cloves
1/2 teaspoon ground cardamom
1/2 teaspoon dry mustard
1 egg
1/2 cup sugar

1/2 cup firmly packed dark brown sugar
1/2 cup (1 stick) unsalted butter (room temperature), cut into 4 pieces
1/4 cup plus 2 tablespoons dark molasses

1/2 cup powdered sugar
Currants, pine nuts, cinnamon candies (optional decorations)

Combine first 11 ingredients in processor and blend well, about 5 seconds. Transfer flour mixture to medium bowl and set aside. Mix egg and sugars in work bowl 1 minute. Add butter and mix 1 minute. Add molasses and blend 15 seconds. Return flour mixture to work bowl and mix using on/off turns just until flour is incorporated; do not overprocess. Transfer dough to plastic bag and flatten into disc. Seal tightly and chill at least 4 hours, preferably overnight.

Position rack in center of oven and preheat to 350°F. Divide dough into 4 equal portions; return 3 to refrigerator. Lightly dust work surface with powdered sugar. Roll 1 portion of dough out to thickness of 1/4 inch. Cut out cookies using 1 1/2-inch round cutter. Arrange on baking sheet, spacing 1 inch apart. Repeat with remaining dough. Decorate cookies as desired. Bake until browned, about 12 minutes. Transfer cookies to wire rack and let cool. Store in airtight container.

A 5-inch gingerbread man cutter can be used. Yield will be about 22 cookies.

Brandied Pfeffernüsse

Makes about 3¹/₂ dozen

1²/₃ cups all purpose flour
1¹/₄ teaspoons baking powder
 1 teaspoon cinnamon
 ¹/₂ teaspoon ground ginger
 ¹/₄ teaspoon allspice
 ¹/₄ teaspoon ground cloves
 ¹/₈ teaspoon ground cardamom
 ¹/₈ teaspoon freshly ground white pepper (optional)
 ¹/₃ cup minced candied lemon peel (3 ounces)
 ¹/₄ cup slivered almonds, minced (1 ounce)
 2 tablespoons minced candied orange peel

 1 medium egg
 ¹/₂ cup sugar
 3 tablespoons brandy
 1 teaspoon vanilla
   Grated peel of 1 medium lemon
 ¹/₈ teaspoon grated orange peel

Brandy Glaze
 1 cup sifted powdered sugar
 1 tablespoon brandy
2¹/₂ to 3 teaspoons (about) hot water
 ¹/₂ teaspoon fresh lemon juice

Sift flour, baking powder and spices; set aside. Toss candied lemon peel, almonds and candied orange peel in small bowl. Beat egg in medium bowl of electric mixer at medium speed 1 minute. Gradually add sugar, brandy, vanilla and grated peels and beat 2 minutes. Reduce mixer speed to low and gradually blend in sifted dry ingredients. Stir in almond mixture. Refrigerate dough for 10 minutes.

Preheat oven to 375°F. Grease baking sheets. Dust work surface generously with flour. Press or roll dough out slightly less than ¹/₂ inch thick, lifting frequently and dusting with flour as necessary to prevent sticking. Cut out cookies using 1¹/₂-inch round cutter, lightly flouring cutter occasionally. Arrange cookies on prepared baking sheets, spacing ¹/₂ inch apart. Bake until tops of cookies just begin to color, about 13 to 15 minutes. Let cool several minutes, then transfer to racks to cool completely before glazing.

For glaze: Mix powdered sugar, brandy, 2¹/₂ teaspoons hot water and lemon juice in small bowl until smooth. Stir in additional water a few drops at a time if necessary until mixture is glaze consistency. Using knife or pastry brush, lightly coat top and sides of each cookie with glaze. Let stand on rack set over waxed paper until glaze is set. Transfer to airtight container to mellow for 2 days before serving. (*Pfeffernüsse can be stored in airtight container for 2 months or frozen indefinitely.*)

Bizcochitos

This dainty anise cookie is traditional in New Mexico at Christmas.

Makes about 6 dozen 3-inch cookies

 4 cups (or more) unbleached all purpose flour
 2 teaspoons baking powder
 ¹/₂ teaspoon salt
1¹/₂ cups solid vegetable shortening
 1 cup sugar
 1 egg

 1 egg yolk
 1 tablespoon aniseed
 ¹/₂ cup dry white wine or water

 ¹/₂ cup sugar
 ¹/₂ teaspoon cinnamon

Sift 4 cups flour, baking powder and salt together. Using electric mixer, cream shortening until light and fluffy. Add 1 cup sugar and beat until fluffy. Blend egg and yolk, then mix into shortening with aniseed. Mix in dry ingredients alternately with wine, adding more flour if necessary to form dough that pulls away from sides of bowl. Gather dough into ball; flatten into disc. Wrap dough tightly and refrigerate until well chilled.

Position rack in upper third of oven and preheat to 400°F. Grease baking sheets. Combine ½ cup sugar and cinnamon in small bowl. Roll dough out on lightly floured surface to thickness of ¼ inch. Cut with decorative cookie cutters. Place on prepared sheets. Gather scraps, reroll and cut additional cookies. Bake cookies until beginning to color, about 15 minutes. Transfer to racks. Immediately sprinkle with cinnamon sugar. Cool.

Whole Wheat English Biscuits

Makes about 5 dozen

2 cups whole wheat flour
2 cups rolled oats
½ cup firmly packed light brown sugar
1 teaspoon baking powder
⅛ teaspoon salt

½ cup (1 stick) well-chilled unsalted butter
½ cup milk
1 egg, room temperature

Combine flour, oats, sugar, baking powder and salt in large bowl. Cut in butter until coarse meal forms. Mix milk and egg. Add to flour mixture and stir until dough begins to gather together, using fork. Wrap in plastic and refrigerate 30 minutes.

Preheat oven to 350°F. Line baking sheets with parchment; grease paper. Cut dough into 4 pieces. Roll 1 piece out on lightly floured surface to a thickness of ¼ inch. Cut out 2-inch rounds. Transfer to prepared sheets. Pierce all over with fork. Repeat with remaining dough. Gather scraps, reroll and cut additional cookies. Bake until golden brown, about 13 minutes. Cool on rack. Store in airtight container.

Caraway Petticoat Tails

Delicious with slices of cheddar cheese.

Makes 8

1½ cups all purpose flour
1 tablespoon caraway seed
½ teaspoon baking powder
½ teaspoon salt
¾ cup (1½ sticks) unsalted butter, melted

¼ cup whipping cream
¼ cup sugar
Powdered sugar (optional)

Preheat oven to 350°F. Lightly grease baking sheet. Combine flour, caraway seed, baking powder and salt in medium bowl. Make well in center. Add butter, cream and ¼ cup sugar to well. Mix just until dough gathers into ball. Gently knead on lightly floured surface just until smooth. Roll out on prepared sheet to 10-inch round. Pierce all over with fork. Cut into 8 wedges, leaving in place. Bake until crisp and golden brown, 20 to 25 minutes. Cool 15 minutes on sheet. Transfer to rack and cool completely. Dust with powdered sugar, if desired. Recut wedges if necessary. Store in airtight container.

Mostaccioli (Mustaches)

A Neapolitan specialty, these cookies are made almost entirely of ground nuts. Mostaccioli are best the day after baking.

Makes about 2¹/₂ dozen

1 cup hazelnuts (about 4 ounces)
1 cup walnuts (4 ounces)
¹/₃ cup honey
1 egg white
1 tablespoon unsweetened cocoa powder
¹/₂ teaspoon cinnamon
¹/₈ teaspoon ground cloves
Pinch of salt
¹/₃ cup all purpose flour

Powdered sugar

Icing
¹/₂ cup powdered sugar, sifted
1 tablespoon egg white, beaten to blend
1 to 2 teaspoons orange liqueur

Preheat oven to 275°F. Grease baking sheet. Finely grind nuts in processor. Add honey, egg white, cocoa, spices and salt and blend to paste. Add flour and mix using on/off turns until just incorporated (dough will be sticky).

Place dough on work surface heavily dusted with sifted powdered sugar. Sift more sugar over dough. Gently roll dough out to thickness of ³/₈ inch. Cut into 1 × 1¹/₂-inch bars using knife dusted with powdered sugar. Arrange on prepared sheet, spacing 1 inch apart. Bake cookies until firm and tops appear dry, 25 to 30 minutes. Cool cookies completely on racks.

For icing: Blend ¹/₂ cup powdered sugar and egg white. Mix in enough liqueur to make thick but pourable icing.

Set racks on waxed paper; arrange cooled cookies on racks with edges touching. Drizzle icing over cookies in irregular lines. Separate cookies. Let stand until icing is dry. Store Mostaccioli in airtight container.

Sweet Semolina Diamonds

Semolina flour, made from durum wheat, is the basis of many pastas. It is combined here with sugar and all purpose flour to produce a slightly sweet, crunchy rum-raisin cookie.

Makes about 3 dozen

1 cup light rum
1 cup seedless golden raisins

4 egg yolks, room temperature
1 cup sugar

2 cups all purpose flour
1¹/₂ cups semolina flour

1 cup (2 sticks) unsalted butter, melted and cooled
1 teaspoon vanilla
Grated peel of 1 lemon
¹/₄ teaspoon salt
¹/₂ cup pine nuts
2 tablespoons powdered sugar

Combine rum and raisins in small bowl and set aside several hours (or overnight) to plump. Drain raisins, reserving liquid. Pat raisins dry.

Preheat oven to 375°F. Generously butter baking sheets. Beat yolks and sugar in large bowl of electric mixer until slowly dissolving ribbon forms when beaters are lifted, 7 minutes.

Combine flours and gradually mix into egg mixture. Blend in melted butter, vanilla, lemon peel, salt and reserved raisin liquid. Fit mixer with dough hook or turn dough out onto lightly floured surface. Knead until smooth, about 5 minutes. Sprinkle raisins and nuts over dough and continue kneading just until incorporated. Lightly flour work surface again. Roll dough out to thickness of ¹/₃ inch. Using very sharp knife, cut dough diagonally into 2-inch-wide strips, then cut diagonally in opposite directions to form diamonds. Transfer diamonds to baking sheets, spacing evenly. Bake until cookies are lightly colored, about 20 minutes. Serve warm or at room temperature. Store in airtight container. Sprinkle with powdered sugar before serving.

Gialletti (Little Yellow Diamonds)

These sturdy golden cookies feature cornmeal, a northern Italian staple. For finest texture, grind cornmeal in processor four to five minutes.

Makes about 4 dozen

1/2 cup golden raisins
1/2 cup dark rum

1/2 cup sugar
2 egg yolks
2/3 cup butter, melted
2 teaspoons grated lemon peel
1 teaspoon vanilla
Pinch of salt

1 1/3 cups all purpose flour
1 cup fine yellow cornmeal
1/3 cup pine nuts

Powdered sugar

Combine raisins and rum in small bowl. Cover and let stand overnight.

Preheat oven to 375°F. Drain raisins well (discarding rum); chop coarsely. Beat sugar and yolks with electric mixer at low speed until blended. Increase speed to high and beat until pale yellow and slowly dissolving ribbon forms when beaters are lifted, about 7 minutes. Beat in butter in thin stream. Blend in lemon peel, vanilla and salt. Using wooden spoon, stir in raisins, flour, cornmeal and pine nuts. Let dough rest about 10 minutes.

Roll dough out on wooden surface to thickness of 1/2 inch. Cut into diamonds with 1-inch sides. Arrange on ungreased baking sheet, spacing 1 inch apart. Reroll scraps and cut additional cookies. Bake until golden, about 15 minutes. Transfer to racks. Cool completely. Dust cookies with powdered sugar just before serving.

❦ Filled Cookies

Half-Moon Cookies

Dainty accompaniments to a cup of tea. The potato flour makes a very tender crust. These are best eaten the same day they are baked, but prepare the dough one day ahead.

Makes about 40

1 3/4 cups (or more) unbleached all
purpose flour
1/2 cup potato flour
1/3 cup sugar
1/2 cup plus 5 tablespoons well-
chilled butter, cut into 1/2-inch
pieces
1 egg

1/2 cup (about) strawberry preserves
1/3 cup pearl sugar* or coarsely
crushed sugar cubes
1/3 cup finely chopped pecans,
walnuts, or brazil nuts
1 egg white, beaten to blend (glaze)

Sift 1 3/4 cups unbleached flour, potato flour and 1/3 cup sugar into processor. Cut in butter until coarse meal forms. Add egg and process just until dough begins to gather together. Gather dough into ball; flatten to disc. Wrap in plastic and refrigerate overnight.

Divide dough in half and soften at room temperature.

Position rack in center of oven and preheat to 350°F. Line baking sheets with parchment. Knead dough briefly to soften, adding more flour if too sticky to work. Roll 1 piece of dough out between sheets of floured waxed paper to thickness of 1/8 inch, refrigerating occasionally if too soft to roll. Cut out 2 1/4- to 2 1/2-inch rounds, using fluted cookie cutter or tart molds. Transfer to prepared sheet. Repeat with remaining piece of dough. Gather scraps, reroll and cut additional cookies. Place 1/4 teaspoon preserves in center of each cookie. Gently fold half of cookie over preserves, covering ²/₃ of bottom half of cookie. Combine pearl sugar and nuts. Brush cookies lightly with glaze. Sprinkle generously with nut mixture. Bake until pale golden, about 10 minutes. Cool on baking sheets 10 minutes. Transfer cookies to rack and cool completely.

* Available at Scandinavian shops and through specialty mail-order catalogs.

Poilâne's Sablé Cookies

Poilâne bakery in Paris is famous not just for its crusty country bread but for its buttery sablés *as well. These simple cookies are sandwiched with fruit jam for a lovely teatime treat.*

Makes 40 sandwiches

1 cup (2 sticks) unsalted butter, room temperature
1 cup sugar
2 eggs, beaten to blend
4 cups unbleached all purpose flour

1 cup (or more) fruit jam (such as raspberry, strawberry or apricot)
Powdered sugar (optional)

Using electric mixer, beat butter until soft. Add sugar and beat until light and fluffy. Blend in eggs, scraping down sides of bowl. Add flour and mix until dough just comes together. Wrap in plastic and refrigerate until firm, at least 2 hours or overnight.

Preheat oven to 350°F. Line baking sheets with parchment paper. Divide dough in half. Roll out 1 piece on lightly floured surface to thickness of ¹/₈ inch. Cut out rounds using 2¹/₂-inch fluted cutter. Gather scraps and refrigerate. Repeat rolling and cutting with remaining dough. Gather scraps and refrigerate. Using small round cutter or top of metal pastry tip, cut out 2 to 3 holes in *half* of rounds. Gather scraps. Press all scraps together. Reroll and cut out additional rounds. Cut out 2 to 3 holes in *half* of rounds. Arrange all rounds on prepared sheets. Bake until dough is set and edges are golden, 10 to 15 minutes. Cool completely on rack.

Spread thin layer of jam on cookies without holes. Top with cookies with holes, pressing gently. If necessary, spoon more jam into holes. Dust with powdered sugar if desired.

Little Rascals

German-style Spitzbuben have a star, heart or other decorative shape cut out of the top of the sandwich; the Swiss version has three tiny holes that reveal the brightly colored filling.

Makes about 3¹/₂ dozen sandwich cookies

1³/₄ cups plus 2 tablespoons all purpose flour
¹/₈ teaspoon salt
³/₄ cup (1¹/₂ sticks) unsalted butter, room temperature
¹/₂ cup sugar

¹/₂ teaspoon vanilla
1 cup slivered almonds, finely ground (4¹/₂ ounces)
¹/₄ cup (about) red raspberry jelly
¹/₂ cup (about) powdered sugar

Sift flour and salt; set aside. Cream butter in medium bowl of electric mixer at medium speed. Add sugar and beat until light and fluffy. Blend in vanilla. Gradually add sifted ingredients, beating until smooth. Fold in almonds. Form dough into ball. Wrap in plastic; flatten into disc. Chill 45 minutes.

Preheat oven to 350°F. Grease baking sheets. Dust work surface and rolling pin generously with flour. Keeping half of dough refrigerated, roll out remainder to thickness of ¹/₈ inch, patching any tears with fingers. (Dough can also be rolled out between sheets of plastic wrap or waxed paper.) Cut out cookies using 1³/₄- to 2-inch scalloped or sawtooth-edged round cutter. Transfer to prepared baking sheets. Repeat with remaining dough. Leave half of circles plain for cookie bottoms. To make tops from remaining circles, cut star, heart or other shape from centers using miniature cutters, or cut three 3/8-inch or smaller round holes in triangular pattern using thimble. Lift out dough trimmings with point of paring knife. Bake cookies until pale gold, about 8 to 10 minutes. Transfer to racks and cool 10 minutes.

Meanwhile, melt jelly over hot water until liquefied, stirring occasionally.

Sift powdered sugar over cookie tops. Place about 1/3 teaspoon of jelly onto center of each cookie bottom, then firmly but gently press top onto jelly to form sandwich. Let cookies cool completely. Store in airtight container up to 4 days; do not freeze cookies.

Linzer Cookies

Makes about 2 dozen cookies

1 1/4 cups whole wheat pastry flour	1 1/2 egg yolks
2 teaspoons cinnamon	2 tablespoons light honey
1/2 teaspoon freshly grated nutmeg	1 teaspoon vanilla
1/4 teaspoon ground cardamom	1/4 cup Raspberry Jam Syrup*
1/4 cup (1/2 stick) unsalted butter	

Combine flour, cinnamon, nutmeg and cardamom in processor and mix well. Add butter and blend using on/off turns until mixture resembles coarse meal. Combine egg yolks, honey and vanilla in small bowl. Add to flour mixture and blend until combined but crumbly. Gather into ball.

Preheat oven to 350°F. Roll dough out between 2 sheets of floured waxed paper to thickness of 3/16 inch. Cut into rounds using 1 1/2-inch cookie cutter. Set half of rounds aside. Cut centers out of remaining rounds using 1/2-inch-diameter plain pastry tip, forming rings. Repeat rolling and cutting using excess pastry and dough cut from centers. Arrange dough rounds and rings on baking sheet. Bake 15 minutes. Let cool. Spread rounds with Raspberry Jam Syrup. Arrange rings on top. Chill until jam sets. Store in airtight container in cool, dark place.

*Raspberry Jam Syrup

Use as a filling for Linzer Cookies or as a spread for toast or muffins.

Makes 1/4 cup

1/4 cup seedless honey-sweetened red or black raspberry jam	1 teaspoon fresh lemon juice

Combine jam and lemon juice in small saucepan over medium heat and stir until jam is melted. Let cool to room temperature before using.

Walnut Linzer Cookies

This dough freezes so well you can have "instant" cookies on hand the year round.

Makes 9 to 10 dozen cookies

4 cups all purpose flour (or more)
4 cups finely ground walnuts (about 1 pound)
2 cups sugar
2 cups (4 sticks) unsalted butter, room temperature
2 eggs

1 (generous) teaspoon vanilla
  Finely grated peel of 1 large lemon

1 10-ounce jar seedless red raspberry jam
  Powdered sugar

Combine 4 cups flour, walnuts, sugar, butter, eggs, vanilla and lemon peel in large bowl and mix thoroughly, adding more flour as necessary to make dough pliable.

Divide dough into 5 portions (for easy storage). Roll each into cylinder 1½ to 2 inches in diameter. Wrap each roll in aluminum foil and refrigerate until firm.

Preheat oven to 350°F. Slice 1 cylinder into ¼-inch rounds. Arrange on ungreased baking sheet (do not crowd as cookies will spread slightly during baking). Bake until medium brown, about 15 minutes. Immediately transfer cookies to waxed paper-covered work surface using spatula. Let cool. Repeat with remaining cylinders.

Before serving, spread raspberry jam over 1 cookie and top with another. Sprinkle with sugar. Repeat with remaining cookies.

4 ❦ Specialty Cookies

Specialty cookies are particularly fancy special-occasion cookies, or ones that may require special equipment. If you've been wondering what to do with the hand-carved Belgian cookie mold that's been adorning the wall since Aunt Sally gave it to you last year, take a look at the classic Speculaas recipe (page 56). Unpack the cookie press tucked away in the cupboard to make the Special Butter Cookies (page 56), delicious ten-inch ribbons that will make a tasty conversation piece over coffee after an elegant dinner.

Simple things such as ice cream, sorbet or fruit become elegant desserts when the cup that holds them is actually a cookie. A *pizzelle* iron fashions the cookie cones for the fanciful Ice Cream Trumpettes (page 59). On the other hand, the Walnut Crisps (page 57) and the Sunshine Coupé (page 58), require no other equipment than an overturned jar for forming cookies hot from the oven.

Sandwich cookies make a lovely dessert. Try putting together a batch of delicate Lemon Ladyfinger Sandwiches (page 62) for a weekend luncheon. On a more whimsical note, Butterscotch and Oatmeal Cookie Ice Cream Sandwiches (page 62), are winners with adults as well as kids.

If you've ever wanted to create those luscious cookies called macaroons, we include helpful hints to make them easy. After you taste the Classic Almond Macaroons (page 64), you'll want to try variations such as chocolate (page 65), pecan (page 66) or Light Macaroons with Lemon-Almond Filling (page 66).

Whether you need a fancy showstopper or simply want to master a new technique, you will find terrific ideas in this chapter.

Speculaas

These crisp spice cookies are shaped with a traditional wooden Belgian mold that leaves a pattern on top. If speculaas molds are unavailable, use a decorative rolling pin or simply cut the dough into squares or bars.

Makes about 2 dozen 2 × 3-inch cookies

¹/₂ cup (1 stick) unsalted butter, room temperature
1¹/₄ cups firmly packed brown sugar
1 egg, beaten to blend
1 teaspoon Cognac
2 cups all purpose flour
2 teaspoons cinnamon

¹/₂ teaspoon allspice
¹/₂ teaspoon baking powder

1 egg white mixed with 1 tablespoon water

Cream butter in large bowl of electric mixer until light and fluffy. Beat in sugar. Mix in egg and Cognac. Combine remaining ingredients in large bowl. Add dry ingredients to butter mixture in 3 batches, mixing well after each addition. Shape dough into ball; flatten into disc. Wrap in waxed paper or plastic wrap and refrigerate 1 hour. (*Dough can also be prepared in processor.*)

Preheat oven to 350°F. Generously grease baking sheet. Roll dough out on lightly floured surface to thickness of about ¹/₄ inch. Flour wooden speculaas molds. Press molds firmly into dough. Carefully release molds from dough. Cut dough from around molds. Using spatula, transfer cookies to prepared sheet, spacing 1 inch apart. Brush cookies lightly with egg white mixture. Bake until very lightly browned, 10 to 15 minutes. Cool cookies on rack.

Special Butter Cookies

Ten-inch-long ribbon cookies are fun to make and delicious to eat.

Makes about 3¹/₂ dozen

2 cups (4 sticks) unsalted butter, room temperature
2 cups sugar
2 eggs

1 tablespoon vanilla
¹/₂ teaspoon salt
5 cups sifted all purpose flour

Preheat oven to 375°F. Using electric mixer, cream butter and sugar until light. Mix in eggs, vanilla and salt. Using spoon, stir in flour. Transfer dough to cookie press fitted with ribbon attachment. Press dough onto ungreased baking sheets in 10-inch-long strips. Bake until golden brown, 8 to 10 minutes. Transfer to racks and cool. Store in airtight container.

Fruit Sticks

Makes about 3 dozen

4 egg yolks
¹/₄ cup light honey
2 teaspoons vanilla
³/₄ cup sifted whole wheat pastry flour

¹/₂ cup chopped walnuts
¹/₂ cup raisins
¹/₂ cup chopped apricots *or* dates

Preheat oven to 300°F. Line baking sheet with waxed paper; oil paper. Beat yolks in large bowl of electric mixer until foamy. Add honey and beat until frothy. Mix in vanilla. Fold in flour. Stir in walnuts, raisins and apricots. Transfer mixture to pastry bag with ¹/₂- to ³/₄-inch opening (do *not* use pastry tube). Pipe out strips of dough to width of baking sheet, spacing about 4 inches apart. Bake 25 to 30 minutes. Cool on wire rack. Cut strips into 2-inch lengths. Store in airtight container.

Clockwise from top: Lemon Hearts; Triple Layer Bars; Coconut Squares; Chocolate Apricot Bars; Viennese Coffee Cones; Indianerkraphen

Brian Leatart

At left: Brownies with Peanut Butter and Caramel Filling; Molasses Jumbos with Ginger Filling; Almond Butterballs with Tart Apricot Filling; Vanilla Crescents with Pistachio Filling; at right: Lemon Ladyfinger Sandwiches; Butter Cookie Cups with Chocolate-Almond Filling; Orange Shortbread Wedges with Mincemeat Filling

Sunshine Coupé

Hazelnut Chocolate Chunk Brownies
Special Butter Cookies

Paul Elson

From top to bottom: Fruit- and Chocolate-filled Cookie Rolls (Cucidati); Sardinian Raisin and Nut Cookies (Papassinos); Orange Wafers (Gallettine all'Arancia); Gialletti (Little Yellow Diamonds); Mostaccioli (Mustaches); Butterballs (Pallottole al Burro); Fave Dolci (Sweet Beans); Biscotti di Regina (Queen's Cookies); Hazelnut Cookies (Biscottini di Nocciole); Sweet Ravioli (Ravioli Dolci); Brutti ma Buoni (Ugly but Good); more sugar-dusted Butterballs

Oatmeal-Molasses Lace Cookies with
Lemon-Buttercream Filling; Half-Moon
Cookies; Toscaboard; Berry Pizzas;
Cardamom Cookies

Walnut Crisps

Shape each fanciful cookie "cup" over the top of a small spice bottle. These are best served the same day they are baked.

Makes about 18

3/4 cup sugar
3 tablespoons unsalted butter
2 tablespoons milk

1 cup finely chopped walnuts
2 tablespoons all purpose flour

Preheat oven to 375°F. Cut out enough 6-inch squares of parchment to line baking sheet. Heat sugar, butter and milk in heavy small saucepan over low heat, stirring until sugar dissolves. Increase heat and bring mixture to boil. Remove from heat and stir in remaining ingredients. Spoon 1 tablespoon batter into center of each parchment square; spread evenly to 1/8-inch-thick circle. Bake until cookies are golden brown, about 7 minutes. Cool 1 1/2 minutes. One at a time, turn paper with cookie attached over top of 1 1/2-inch-diameter bottles and gently press to form cups. Cool until firm, about 5 minutes. Remove paper and cool cookies completely on rack. Repeat with remaining batter.

Walnut Pastry Cups with Poached Oranges
(Galettes Renversées aux Noix avec Oranges Pochées)

Fill these delicate cookies with lemon sorbet and almond ice cream.

4 servings

Oranges
4 small navel oranges

2 quarts water
1/2 cup sugar
3 tablespoons whole black peppercorns
1 vanilla bean, split

Pastry Cups
1 egg white
1/4 cup sugar
2 tablespoons cake flour

Pinch of salt
2 tablespoons (1/4 stick) unsalted butter, melted and cooled
1/4 teaspoon vanilla
3 tablespoons ground walnuts

2/3 cup lemon sorbet
2/3 cup almond, orange or banana ice cream

For oranges: Remove peel from 1 orange (colored part only). Cut into fine julienne. Boil 4 minutes. Drain and set aside. Remove peel from remaining oranges (colored part only) and reserve. Discard white pith from all oranges.

Cook water, sugar, peppercorns and vanilla bean in heavy large non-aluminum saucepan until sugar dissolves, swirling pan occasionally. Increase heat and bring to simmer. Add *nonjulienned* orange peels and boil until liquid is syrupy but not too thick, about 35 minutes.

Strain syrup into bowl. Add orange peel julienne and oranges. Cover and refrigerate until ready to serve.

For pastry cups: Position rack in center of oven and preheat to 425°F. Butter and flour baking sheet. Trace four 5-inch rounds on sheet. Whisk white, sugar, flour and salt in small bowl until smooth. Whisk in butter and vanilla. Stir in walnuts. Spread approximately 1 1/2 tablespoons batter in each round. Bake until pale golden and browned around edges, turning sheet once for even baking, 6 to 7 minutes. Let stand 1 1/2 to 2 minutes on sheet. Remove immediately and mold over inverted jars to form pastry cups.

Cover dessert plates with orange syrup. Set pastry cups in center. Fill with 1 scoop sorbet and 1 scoop ice cream. Top with orange. Sprinkle with candied orange peel julienne.

Butter Cookie Cups with Chocolate-Almond Filling

*These make elegant after-
dinner treats.*

Makes about 3 dozen

Cookie Cups
- 1 cup plus 2 tablespoons sifted all
  purpose flour
- 3 tablespoons plus 1 1/2 teaspoons
  sugar
- 1/4 teaspoon salt
- 6 tablespoons (3/4 stick) well-chilled
  unsalted butter, cut into 1/2-inch
  cubes
- 1 egg yolk
- 1/2 teaspoon vanilla
- 1/8 teaspoon almond extract

Filling
- 3 tablespoons almond paste
- 6 tablespoons whipping cream
- 6 ounces semisweet chocolate,
  broken into pieces
- 3 tablespoons unsalted butter, room
  temperature
- 3 tablespoons amaretto liqueur
- 1/4 teaspoon vanilla

For cookies: Blend flour, sugar and salt in processor. Cut in butter until coarse
meal forms, using on/off turns. Add yolk, vanilla and almond extract. Process
until mixture gathers together. Form dough into 1-inch-diameter log on plastic
wrap. Wrap tightly and refrigerate until well chilled, about 3 hours. (*Can be
prepared 2 days ahead.*)

Set rack in lowest position of oven and preheat to 350°F. Butter 1 3/4 ×
3/4-inch round tartlet pans. Cut dough into scant 1/4-inch-thick slices. Press one
slice into each pan. Arrange cookie cups on baking sheet. Bake until golden
brown, about 15 minutes. Cool 5 minutes on rack. Gently remove cookies
from pans and cool completely on rack. (*Can be prepared 1 day ahead. Store
in airtight container.*)

For filling: Using fork, mash almond paste into cream in heavy medium
skillet. Add chocolate. Stir over low heat until chocolate melts. Remove from
heat. Mix in butter 1 tablespoon at a time. Stir until lukewarm. Mix in amaretto
and vanilla. Cover filling with paper towel and plastic wrap. Refrigerate until
just firm, about 1 hour.

Spoon filling into pastry bag fitted with medium star tip (no. 6). Pipe filling
into cups 1/3 inch above rims. Refrigerate at least 1 1/2 hours (*Can be prepared 6
hours ahead.*) Serve chilled.

Sunshine Coupé

*Delicate cookie cups hold a
lemon sherbet. The recipe
yields extra cookie cups to
allow for breakage.*

8 servings

Lemon Sherbet
- 2 cups water
- 1 cup sugar
- 2 tablespoons grated lemon peel
- 3/4 cup fresh lemon juice
- 2 egg whites, room temperature

Cookie Cups
- 1/2 cup sugar
- 1/3 cup unsalted butter, room
  temperature
- 2 teaspoons grated lemon peel

- 1/4 teaspoon vanilla
- 2 egg whites, room temperature,
  beaten to blend
- 1/2 cup sifted all purpose flour

- 2 oranges
- 1 pint strawberries, halved
- 1/4 cup strawberry preserves
- 1 tablespoon kirsch

  Mint sprigs

For sherbet: Cook water, sugar and lemon peel in heavy small saucepan over low
heat, swirling pan occasionally, until sugar dissolves. Increase heat and boil
1 minute. Cool completely. Strain syrup, discarding lemon peel. Mix in lemon

juice. Beat whites until stiff but not dry. Fold into syrup. Process mixture in ice cream maker according to manufacturer's instructions. Freeze in covered container several hours to mellow flavors.

For cookies: Preheat oven to 400°F. Cut out twelve 7-inch foil squares. Butter foil. Trace 6-inch circle on each, using bamboo skewer or knife. Lightly butter back of two 3- to 3½-inch-diameter bowls or custard cups. Using electric mixer, beat sugar, butter, lemon peel and vanilla until very fluffy. Mix in whites. Fold in flour.

Place 2 foil squares on baking sheet. Spoon 1½ tablespoons batter into center of each circle; spread evenly to edges of circles. Bake until edges of cookies are golden brown, 5 to 7 minutes. Immediately invert each over back of prepared bowl; press to form cup shape. Let stand until firm, about 10 seconds. Gently peel off foil and remove cookies from bowls. Repeat with remaining batter.

Remove peel and white pith from oranges. Cut between membranes with small sharp knife to release segments. Combine orange segments with strawberries in medium bowl. Melt preserves in heavy small saucepan. Strain into small bowl. Stir in kirsch. Mix into fruit and let stand 10 minutes.

Spoon sherbet into cookie cups. Top with fruit. Garnish with mint and serve immediately.

Ice Cream Trumpettes

A pizzelle iron is necessary to make the cone for this fanciful dessert. There is enough batter to allow for breakage.

8 servings

3 ounces hazelnuts, toasted and husked
²/₃ cup sugar

1 cup whipping cream
½ teaspoon vanilla
1 cup all purpose flour
1 cup powdered sugar

2 tablespoons (about) butter, melted

6 ounces bittersweet or semisweet chocolate, coarsely ground
Chocolate ice cream
Vanilla ice cream

Arrange hazelnuts on well-oiled heatproof surface or baking sheet. Heat sugar in heavy small skillet over medium heat until dissolved and caramelized to medium golden, swirling pan occasionally, about 5 minutes. Pour over hazelnuts. Cool completely. Break praline into pieces. Coarsely grind in processor using on/off turns.

In large bowl beat cream with vanilla to stiff peaks. Using spatula, gently fold in flour and powdered sugar; do not overfold. Cover batter and refrigerate for 30 minutes.

Heat pizzelle iron over medium-high heat. Brush both sides with some of butter. Remove from heat. Spoon generous tablespoon batter in center of iron. Close iron. Return to heat and cook batter 1 minute. Turn iron over and cook second side until medium golden, about 1 minute. Using small spoon as aid, immediately remove pizzelle from iron and fit into (not around) Champagne flute or cannoli mold. Cool completely. Remove from flute. (*Can be prepared 1 day ahead and stored in airtight container in cool dry place.*) Repeat with remaining batter, wiping crumbs from iron and brushing with butter each time.

Cover half of dessert plate with chocolate and half with praline (about 2 to 3 tablespoons each). Place 1 scoop chocolate ice cream on chocolate and 1 scoop vanilla ice cream on praline. Place 1 pizzelle on each scoop, pointed end up. Serve immediately.

Viennese Coffee Cones

*Elegant confections to serve
with espresso. The cream
horn or "lady lock" form
used to shape the cookies
can be found at
cookware stores.*

Makes about 18

Cookie Cones
 2 egg whites, room temperature
 8 tablespoons sugar
 1/4 cup (1/2 stick) unsalted butter,
    melted and cooled
 4 1/2 teaspoons all purpose flour
 1/2 teaspoon vanilla

Coffee-Cinnamon Cream Filling
 1 teaspoon unflavored gelatin
 3 tablespoons cold water

 4 1/2 teaspoons Kahlúa or other coffee
    liqueur
 1 1/2 teaspoons instant coffee powder
 3/8 teaspoon vanilla
 1/4 teaspoon (scant) cinnamon
 1 1/2 cups well-chilled whipping cream
 6 tablespoons powdered sugar

 Chocolate coffee bean candies

For cookies: Preheat oven to 350°F. Grease and flour 6-inch-wide strip down center of nonstick baking sheet. Trace two 5-inch circles in flour. Blend egg whites in processor until light and frothy, about 20 seconds. With machine running, add sugar through feed tube 1 tablespoon at a time. Blend until consistency of whipping cream, about 30 seconds. Scrape down sides of work bowl. Add butter, flour and vanilla. Mix until just blended, using 5 to 6 on/off turns and stopping once to scrape down bowl.

Spread 2 teaspoons batter evenly within each circle on prepared sheet. Bake until cookies are uniformly golden brown, 6 to 7 minutes. Cool 30 seconds. Invert 1 cookie onto work surface, using metal spatula. Immediately form cone by rolling cookie around cream horn or lady lock form. Press edges to seal. Transfer to rack. Repeat with second cookie, returning to oven briefly if too firm to form. Repeat with remaining batter, rinsing, buttering and flouring baking sheet between batches. Let cookies cool. Transfer cookies to airtight container.

For filling: Soften gelatin in cold water in small bowl. Place bowl in pan of simmering water and stir until gelatin is dissolved. Add liqueur, coffee, vanilla and cinnamon and stir until coffee dissolves. Using electric mixer, beat cream and powdered sugar until soft peaks form. Beat in gelatin mixture; continue beating until stiff. (*Can be prepared 8 hours ahead and chilled.*)

Just before serving, spoon filling into pastry bag fitted with large star tip. Pipe cream into cones. Top each with chocolate coffee bean candy.

Strawberry Bavarians on Sugar Cookies

*A truly spectacular way to
use fresh strawberries is in
the custard for bavarian
creams. These rosy-pink
bavarians, which are
smooth as silk and
lightened with whipped
cream, rest on vanilla-
flavored sugar cookies. The
fresh berries are used in the
sauce, too, in addition to
pureed raspberries.*

8 servings

Strawberry-Raspberry Sauce
 1 pint strawberries
 1 10-ounce package frozen
    raspberries, thawed (undrained)
 1 to 2 tablespoons sugar

Bavarians
 2/3 cup milk

 1 pint strawberries
 4 teaspoons unflavored gelatin
 3/4 cup sugar

 3 egg yolks
 1 tablespoon raspberry preserves
 4 1/2 teaspoons kirsch

 1 cup strawberries, sliced

 1 cup well-chilled whipping cream

 8 Sugar Cookies*

For sauce: Blend strawberries, raspberries in processor with liquid and 1 tablespoon sugar until smooth. Taste and add remaining 1 tablespoon sugar if desired. Strain sauce through fine sieve to remove seeds. Cover and refrigerate until well chilled. (*Sauce can be prepared 4 days ahead.*)

For bavarians: Bring milk to boil in heavy 2-quart saucepan.

Puree 1 pint strawberries in processor until smooth. Transfer to large bowl. Sprinkle gelatin over; stir gently. Process sugar and yolks 1 minute. Add preserves and blend 5 seconds. With machine running, pour hot milk through feed tube and mix 10 seconds. Return to saucepan. Stir over low heat until thick enough to coat spoon and thermometer registers 175°F, about 6 minutes. Immediately add to pureed strawberries and stir until gelatin is completely dissolved. Mix in kirsch. Refrigerate mixture until slightly thickened but not set.

Lightly oil eight ²/₃-cup soufflé dishes. Line bottoms with foil and lightly oil foil. Cover bottoms with sliced berries, arranging in circular pattern.

With machine running, pour cream through processor feed tube and process until thick, about 1 minute; do not overprocess. Gently fold cream into thickened strawberry mixture. Divide among soufflé dishes. Refrigerate 4 hours. (*Can be prepared 1 day ahead.*)

Spoon 2 tablespoons sauce onto 8 plates. Place sugar cookie in center of each. Run small knife around bavarians and invert atop cookies. Rearrange strawberry slices if necessary. Brush tops of bavarians lightly with sauce. Let bavarians stand at room temperature 15 minutes before serving. Pass remaining sauce separately.

*Sugar Cookies

Makes about 12

2 hard-cooked egg yolks
1¹/₃ sticks well-chilled unsalted butter, cut into tablespoon-size pieces
1 cup plus 2 tablespoons unbleached all purpose flour (5¹/₂ ounces)

²/₃ cup powdered sugar (2²/₃ ounces)
1¹/₂ teaspoons vanilla
³/₄ teaspoon cold milk
¹/₈ teaspoon salt

Finely chop yolks in processor. Add all remaining ingredients. Blend using 4 on/off turns, then process continuously until dough begins to gather together; do not form ball. Transfer dough to plastic bag. Shape into ball, then flatten to disc. Refrigerate dough at least 4 hours or overnight.

Position rack in center of oven and preheat to 375°F. Line baking sheet with parchment. Cut dough into 3 pieces. Return 2 to refrigerator. Roll 1 piece out between sheets of plastic wrap to thickness of ³/₁₆ inch. Cut into 3¹/₂-inch fluted rounds, using cookie cutter. Transfer to prepared sheet, spacing 1 inch apart. Repeat with remaining dough. Freeze cookies until firm, about 15 minutes.

Bake cookies until edges are golden brown, about 12 minutes. Transfer parchment and cookies to rack and cool 8 minutes. Remove cookies from parchment, using spatula; cool completely on rack. (*Can be prepared 3 days ahead. Store in airtight container.*)

Lemon Ladyfinger Sandwiches

Makes 18

Lemon Curd
- 2 teaspoons cornstarch
- 1/4 cup fresh lemon juice
- 6 tablespoons sugar
- 3 tablespoons unsalted butter, cubed
- 3 egg yolks, room temperature
- 2 teaspoons finely grated lemon peel
- 1 egg, room temperature

Ladyfingers
- 3 egg yolks, room temperature
- 2 1/2 teaspoons fresh lemon juice
- 1/2 teaspoon vanilla
- 1/2 teaspoon finely grated lemon peel
- 3 egg whites, room temperature
- 2 pinches of salt
- 1/2 cup superfine sugar
- 2/3 cup sifted all purpose flour
- 1/2 cup powdered sugar

For curd: Dissolve cornstarch in lemon juice. Combine remaining ingredients in heavy small skillet. Whisk in dissolved cornstarch. Set over medium-low heat and whisk until thickened and smooth, about 5 minutes. Transfer to bowl. Press plastic wrap directly on surface to prevent skin from forming. Refrigerate. (*Lemon Curd can be prepared 2 days ahead.*)

For ladyfingers: Position rack in center of oven and preheat to 325°F. Dab butter in each corner of 2 baking sheets. Line sheets with foil, allowing 1-inch overhang at short ends. Butter and flour foil, shaking off excess. With long edge of sheet toward you, mark off 3 rows of six 4-inch lines.

Whisk yolks, lemon juice, vanilla and peel in small bowl. Using electric mixer, beat whites and salt to soft peaks. Gradually add superfine sugar and beat until stiff and shiny. Gently fold in yolk mixture. Sift in flour in four additions, folding gently after each. Spoon batter into pastry bag fitted with No. 6 star tip. Pipe 18 ladyfingers onto each sheet, using lines as guides. Sift powdered sugar over ladyfingers. Let stand 2 minutes. Using fingertip, press down points at ends of ladyfingers. Bake until lightly colored and crisp, 17 to 18 minutes. Transfer foil to rack and let stand 15 minutes. Peel ladyfingers off foil and cool completely on rack. Fill within several hours, or layer with paper towels in airtight container and store overnight.

To assemble: Spread 2 teaspoons lemon curd on flat surface of 1 ladyfinger. Press flat surface of another ladyfinger onto lemon curd to form sandwich. Set on platter. Repeat with remaining ladyfingers. Serve immediately.

Butterscotch and Oatmeal Cookie Ice Cream Sandwiches

Makes 12

- 1 cup rolled oats
- 1 cup all purpose flour
- 1 cup firmly packed light brown sugar
- 1/2 cup (1 stick) unsalted butter, melted
- 2 tablespoons boiling water
- 1 tablespoon corn syrup
- 1 1/2 teaspoons baking soda
- 1 teaspoon vanilla

- 1 quart butterscotch ice cream

Preheat oven to 350°F. Lightly grease baking sheets. Mix oatmeal, flour and brown sugar in large bowl. Stir in butter. Blend water, syrup, baking soda and vanilla in another bowl. Add to oatmeal mixture and knead gently until dough comes together. Shape dough into 24 rounds. Arrange rounds on prepared sheets, flattening slightly. Bake until golden brown, about 12 minutes. Transfer to racks and cool. Freeze while preparing ice cream.

Place ice cream in bowl. Stir with wooden spoon until soft enough to be piped; do not allow to melt. Spoon into pastry bag fitted with large star tip. Pipe spiral of ice cream onto 12 cookies. Sandwich with remaining 12 cookies, pressing gently. Arrange on rack and freeze until firm. Store cookies in plastic bags until ready to serve.

Molasses Jumbos with Ginger Filling

Makes about 2 dozen

Molasses Cookies
- 2/3 cup firmly packed light brown sugar
- 1/2 cup light molasses
- 1/2 cup (1 stick) unsalted butter

- 1 extra-large egg
- 1 tablespoon cider vinegar
- 2 teaspoons vanilla
- 3 cups sifted all purpose flour
- 3/4 teaspoon ground ginger
- 3/4 teaspoon baking soda
- 3/4 teaspoon cinnamon
- 1/2 teaspoon salt
- 1/2 teaspoon ground cloves
- 1/4 teaspoon ground cardamom

  Melted butter
  All purpose flour

Ginger Filling
- 2 1/2 cups powdered sugar
- 7 tablespoons chopped crystallized ginger (3 ounces)
- 4 tablespoons ginger marmalade
- 4 tablespoons well-chilled unsalted butter, cut into 4 pieces

For cookies: Stir sugar, molasses and butter in heavy 2- to 3-quart saucepan over low heat until butter melts. Cool mixture to lukewarm.

Stir egg, vinegar and vanilla into molasses mixture. Combine dry ingredients and gradually stir into molasses mixture. Cover and chill 1 1/2 hours to firm. (*Can be prepared 3 days ahead.*)

Invert baking sheets and cover undersides with foil. Brush with melted butter and dust with flour, shaking off excess. Form dough into 1-inch balls. Arrange on foil, spacing 3 inches apart. Flatten each cookie into 3-inch round (saucepan bottom wrapped in plastic works well). Chill 1 1/2 hours.

Preheat oven to 325°F. Bake cookies until honey colored, about 14 minutes. Slide foil onto work surface. Gently press each cookie with spatula to flatten. Cool. (*Can be prepared 2 days ahead. Store in airtight container.*)

For filling: Blend 1 1/4 cups sugar and 3 1/2 tablespoons ginger in processor until ginger is minced, stopping occasionally to scrape down sides of work bowl, about 2 minutes. Add 2 tablespoons marmalade and 2 tablespoons butter. Process until thick and well blended, about 1 1/2 minutes. Transfer mixture to small bowl. Repeat with remaining sugar, ginger, marmalade and butter. Add to bowl. (*Can be prepared 1 day ahead and refrigerated. Bring filling to room temperature before continuing.*)

Spread 1 tablespoon filling on bottom of cookie, smoothing to edges. Press bottom of another cookie firmly onto filling. Repeat with remaining cookies. (*Can be prepared 6 hours ahead. Store uncovered to retain crispness.*)

Gingersnapwiches

Ginger, chocolate and ice cream combine to make this terrific dessert. The shortbread cookie recipe makes enough for the eight large cookies used for the "snapwiches," plus dough to cut more in any size desired.

4 servings

1½ pints rich vanilla ice cream, slightly softened
¼ cup finely minced candied ginger (optional)

8 3-inch-square Ginger Shortbread Cookies*
1 cup miniature chocolate chips

Mix ice cream and ginger. Divide among 4 cookies, spreading to edges. Top with remaining cookies. Roll edges in chocolate chips (freeze several minutes if ice cream is too soft). Wrap in plastic and freeze until firm. (*Can be prepared 1 day ahead.*) Serve frozen.

*Ginger Shortbread Cookies

1 cup (2 sticks) unsalted butter, room temperature
¾ cup sugar
1¾ cups all purpose flour
¼ cup cornstarch
1½ teaspoons ground ginger

1 teaspoon cinnamon
¼ teaspoon ground cloves
¼ teaspoon salt

Additional sugar

Cream butter with ¾ cup sugar, using electric mixer. Sift in remaining ingredients except additional sugar. Mix just until firm dough forms. Wrap tightly and refrigerate 30 minutes.

Preheat oven to 325°F. Roll dough out on lightly floured surface to thickness of ¼ inch. Cut out eight 3-inch squares. Arrange on baking sheet. Cut remaining dough in any shapes desired and arrange on baking sheet. Sprinkle cookies with sugar. Bake until firm and lightly colored, about 20 minutes. Cool completely on racks before filling.

Classic Almond Macaroons

Makes about 20

1½ cups blanched almonds*
1 cup sugar
2 egg whites
¼ teaspoon almond extract

4 teaspoons powdered sugar

Position rack in upper third of oven and preheat to 325°F. Line baking sheet with parchment or waxed paper; butter paper lightly. Finely grind almonds with ¼ cup sugar in processor. Add egg whites and almond extract and blend until smooth, about 20 seconds. Add remaining ¾ cup sugar in 2 batches, blending until smooth after each addition, about 10 seconds.

Roll about 1 tablespoon almond mixture between moistened palms into smooth ball. Transfer to prepared baking sheet. Repeat with remaining mixture, spacing cookies 1 inch apart. Press to flatten each macaroon to ½ inch high. Gently brush surface of each with water. Sift powdered sugar over. Bake until very light brown, about 25 minutes (centers will be soft).

Remove baking sheet from oven. Immediately lift one end of paper and pour 2 tablespoons water onto sheet; water will boil. Lift other end of paper and pour 2 tablespoons water under it. Tilt baking sheet to spread water. When water stops boiling, gently remove macaroons from paper using metal spatula. Cool on rack.

To Blanch Almonds

Bring enough water to generously cover almonds to a boil. Add almonds and boil 10 seconds. Remove 1 almond, using slotted spoon. Press end with thumb and finger; almond should slip out of skin. If not, boil a few seconds longer and try again. When almonds can be peeled easily, drain and peel remainder. Spread blanched almonds in single layer on paper towels. Pat dry. Almonds must be completely dry before grinding.

Chocolate Macaroons

Makes about 35

3 ounces semisweet chocolate, coarsely chopped
1 cup (about 4 ounces) blanched almonds (see recipe above)
²/₃ cup sugar
2 egg whites

Position rack in center of oven and preheat to 325°F. Line 2 baking sheets with parchment or waxed paper; butter paper lightly. Melt chocolate in top of double boiler set over hot but not boiling water. Stir until smooth. Remove from over hot water and cool 3 to 5 minutes (do not let harden). Finely grind almonds with 2 tablespoons sugar in processor, stopping occasionally to scrape down sides of work bowl. Add egg whites and remaining sugar alternately, in 2 batches, blending until smooth after each addition. Transfer to large bowl. Gradually stir in melted chocolate.

Spoon mixture into pastry bag fitted with medium-sized plain tip (¹/₂ inch, No. 6). Pipe mixture onto prepared baking sheets in 1-inch rounds, spacing 1 inch apart. Flatten points if necessary to form smooth round shape. Bake 5 minutes.* Wedge oven door slightly open with handle of wooden spoon. Continue baking until cookies are just firm to touch, about 7 more minutes (centers will be soft).

Remove baking sheet from oven. Immediately lift one end of paper and pour 2 tablespoons water onto sheet; water will boil. Lift other end of paper and pour 2 tablespoons water under it. Tilt baking sheet to spread water. When water stops boiling, gently remove macaroons from paper using metal spatula. Cool on rack.

*If 2 baking sheets do not fit on oven rack, bake macaroons on 2 racks. Halfway through baking time, switch positions of sheets so macaroons will bake evenly.

Southern Hills Macaroons

Makes about 5 dozen

14 ounces almond paste
1³/₄ cups powdered sugar
1 cup granulated sugar
¹/₄ cup white cornmeal
1 tablespoon honey
¹/₂ cup egg whites (about 4 large)

Preheat oven to 350°F. Line baking sheets with parchment paper (do not use waxed paper). Combine almond paste, sugars, cornmeal and honey in large bowl and blend until smooth. Gradually add egg whites, mixing well. Spoon mixture into pastry bag fitted with No. 8 plain round tip. Pipe onto prepared baking sheets in rounds about 1¹/₄ inches in diameter, spacing 1¹/₂ inches apart. Flatten slightly with dampened cloth. Bake until light golden, about 20 to 25 minutes. Slide macaroons (still on parchment) onto racks. Let cool completely, then carefully peel off parchment paper. Store macaroons in airtight container.

If baking sheets will be reused, let cool between batches to avoid scorching bottoms of macaroons.

Pecan Macaroons

Makes about 20

1¹/₂ cups pecan halves
10 tablespoons sugar
 1 egg white

 2 tablespoons firmly packed light brown sugar

Position rack in upper third of oven and preheat to 325°F. Line baking sheet with parchment or waxed paper; butter paper lightly. Set aside 20 pecan halves for garnish. Finely grind remaining pecans with 2 tablespoons sugar in processor, stopping occasionally to scrape down sides of work bowl. Add egg white and mix 10 seconds. Add remaining 8 tablespoons (¹/₂ cup) sugar and mix until smooth, about 15 seconds. Scrape down sides of work bowl. Add brown sugar and mix until smooth, about 10 seconds.

Roll 2 teaspoons pecan mixture between moistened palms into smooth oval, 1¹/₂ × ¹/₂ inches. Transfer to prepared baking sheet. Repeat with remaining mixture, spacing cookies about 1 inch apart. Press to flatten each macaroon to ¹/₂ inch high. Gently brush surface of each with water. Press reserved pecan half into top of each macaroon. Bake until light brown and just firm to the touch, about 20 minutes (centers will be soft).

Remove baking sheet from oven. Immediately lift one end of paper and pour 2 tablespoons water onto sheet; water will boil. Lift other end of paper and pour 2 tablespoons water under it. Tilt baking sheet to spread water. When water stops boiling, gently remove macaroons from paper, using metal spatula. Cool completely on rack.

Light Macaroons with Lemon-Almond Filling

Makes about 40 sandwich cookies

Macaroons
¹/₂ cup sugar
¹/₄ cup water
 4 egg whites

 1 cup plus 2 tablespoons blanched almonds (see page 65)
1¹/₄ cups powdered sugar

Lemon-Almond Filling
1¹/₂ cups blanched almonds
  (see page 65)

1¹/₂ cups powdered sugar
1¹/₂ cups (3 sticks) unsalted butter, room temperature
 2 tablespoons grated lemon peel
 2 tablespoons fresh lemon juice

For macaroons: Position racks in center of 2 ovens; preheat 1 oven to 450°F and second to 350°F.* Line 4 baking sheets with parchment paper; butter paper lightly. Combine ¹/₂ cup sugar and ¹/₄ cup water in heavy small saucepan over low heat. Cook until sugar dissolves, swirling pan occasionally. Increase heat and boil, without stirring, until candy thermometer registers 240°F (soft-ball stage). Meanwhile, beat 2 egg whites in large bowl of electric mixer until stiff but not dry. Gradually pour hot syrup into whites, beating constantly on high. Continue beating until mixture is room temperature, 3 to 4 minutes.

Grind 1 cup plus 2 tablespoons almonds with 2 tablespoons powdered sugar in processor until mixture forms fine crumbs. Add remaining 1 cup plus 2 tablespoons powdered sugar 2 tablespoons at a time, using about 6 on/off turns after each addition until sugar is absorbed. Continue blending 1 minute; do not form paste. Add remaining 2 egg whites and mix just until smooth. Transfer to large bowl. Fold in 1/3 of meringue to lighten mixture. Gently fold in remaining meringue in 2 batches, blending well.

Spoon mixture into pastry bag fitted with small plain tip (3/8 inch, No. 4). Pipe mixture onto prepared baking sheets in 1-inch rounds, spacing 1 1/2 inches apart. Let dry 10 minutes.

🍒 Macaroons

Making delicious macaroons is much easier than you might think. Macaroon batter is simple to put together because it contains only three basic ingredients: ground nuts, egg whites and sugar. The rich flavor of fresh nuts is the star component. Almonds are the most popular, but pecans also make an exquisite cookie, particularly when brown sugar is added for a praline flavor.

The classic macaroon batter becomes foolproof when made with the aid of a food processor or nut grinder. The processor grinds the nuts finely, then blends in egg whites and sugar in a matter of seconds. Alternatively, the nuts can be ground with a nut grinder or hand rotary grater and briefly mixed with the egg whites and sugar in a bowl.

While macaroons require no special equipment or complicated technique, it is important to remember that they are done before they appear to be. The cookies are baked just until light brown, soft in the center and firm enough to be removed from the baking sheet. They might appear too soft, but it is amazing how much they harden as they cool. Also, macaroons are removed from the baking sheets in an unusual way. The parchment paper lining is lifted and water is poured underneath, directly onto the sheet. Upon contact with the hot baking sheet, the water sizzles, releasing the macaroons. The water also creates steam, which helps keep them moist.

Tips
• The nuts must be very finely ground. When using a food processor, grind them with a small amount of sugar in the recipe to prevent their becoming oily and forming nut butter.
• If you do not have a food processor, grind the nuts in small batches in a nut grinder or grate them in a hand rotary grater. A blender will not grind nuts evenly. Transfer the ground nuts to a bowl and stir in the remaining dry ingredients thoroughly. Make a well in the mixture and add the liquid ingredients. Stir, gradually incorporating all of the dry ingredients.
• It is best not to bake macaroons on very humid days because they might become overly sticky.
• Store cooled macaroons in airtight containers for up to 1 week.

Bake 1 or 2 sheets of macaroons in 450°F oven 1 minute.* Transfer to 350°F oven and wedge door open slightly with handle of wooden spoon. Continue baking until macaroons are light brown and just firm, 14 minutes.

Remove baking sheet from oven. Immediately lift one end of paper and pour 2 tablespoons water onto sheet; water will boil. Lift other end of paper and pour 2 tablespoons water under it. Tilt baking sheet to spread water. When water stops boiling, gently remove macaroons from paper using metal spatula. Cool on rack.

For filling: Grind 1½ cups almonds and ¼ cup powdered sugar in processor until coarsely chopped. Add remaining 1¼ cups powdered sugar 2 tablespoons at a time, mixing 10 seconds after each addition. Continue blending until mixture is very fine. Beat butter in large bowl of electric mixer (or use wooden spoon) until light and fluffy. Stir in almond mixture and peel. Gradually add lemon juice.

Spread about 1 teaspoon filling on flat side of 1 macaroon. Place another macaroon flat side down against filling. Smooth filling around edge. Repeat with remaining macaroons. Refrigerate until filling is firm, about 2 hours. (*Macaroons can be prepared 5 days ahead. Wrap in plastic and refrigerate.*)

*Macaroons can be baked in 1 oven. Position rack in center, place oven thermometer in oven and preheat to 450°F. Bake 1 sheet of cookies 1 minute. Turn off oven and open door until thermometer reads 350°F, about 3 minutes. Set oven at 350°F. Wedge door open slightly with handle of wooden spoon. Continue baking for 9 to 10 minutes.

Bolognese Pinwheels

This recipe makes four rolls that are then sliced into pinwheels. Fill each with a different type of jam. The recipe can be halved.

Makes about 40

1 cup (2 sticks) unsalted butter, room temperature
1 cup plus 2 tablespoons sugar
2 extra-large eggs
2½ cups unbleached all purpose flour
2½ teaspoons baking powder
Pinch of salt

1 cup thick fruit jam (sour cherry, fig, strawberry, quince or apricot)

1 egg yolk beaten with 2 teaspoons milk (glaze)

Using electric mixer, cream butter with sugar until fluffy. Beat in eggs 1 at a time. Sift in flour, baking powder and salt. Mix on low speed until just incorporated. Form dough into ball. Wrap in waxed paper and flatten into disc. Refrigerate dough 1 hour.

Position racks in center and upper third of oven and preheat to 375°F. Line 2 baking sheets with parchment. Cut off ¼ of dough; return remainder to refrigerator. Dust piece of dough with flour. Roll out between sheets of waxed paper to 10 × 6-inch rectangle. Free top sheet of waxed paper from dough and then replace lightly. Turn dough over and remove top sheet of paper. Spread scant ¼ cup jam over top of dough, leaving ½-inch border. Roll up jelly roll fashion, starting at one short side. Pinch seams to seal; fold ends under. Place on prepared sheet. Repeat with remaining dough and jam, spacing rolls 5 inches apart.

Brush rolls with glaze. Bake 15 minutes. Rotate sheets and continue baking until rolls are golden brown, about 15 minutes; rolls will spread. Transfer to racks and cool completely. (*Can be prepared 3 days ahead. Store in airtight container.*) Shortly before serving, cut each roll into ¾-inch-thick slices.

Maple-Fig Pinwheels

For crisp cookies, serve these the day they are baked. For chewy ones, serve them one or two days later.

Makes 48

Dough

1³/₄ cups sifted all purpose flour
¹/₂ teaspoon baking powder
¹/₂ teaspoon salt
²/₃ cup sugar
10 tablespoons (1¹/₄ sticks) well-chilled butter, cubed
¹/₄ cup firmly packed dark brown sugar
2 ounces well-chilled cream cheese, cubed
1 egg
1¹/₂ teaspoons finely grated lemon peel
1 teaspoon fresh lemon juice
1 teaspoon vanilla

Filling

10 ounces dried, moist-pack Calimyrna figs, cubed
¹/₂ cup maple syrup
2 tablespoons water
1 tablespoon fresh lemon juice
¹/₂ teaspoon finely grated lemon peel

1 egg white
1¹/₂ teaspoons fresh lemon juice
2 drops of maple extract

For dough: Mix flour, baking powder and salt in large bowl. Cream remaining ingredients in processor using on/off turns, stopping to scrape down sides of bowl. Using fork, work creamed mixture into dry ingredients. Gather dough into ball. Wrap in plastic; flatten into square. Chill overnight.

For filling: Combine figs, maple syrup, water, 1 tablespoon lemon juice and peel in heavy medium saucepan and bring to simmer. Cover and simmer until figs are soft and liquid is thickened, stirring occasionally, about 15 minutes. Cool 15 minutes.

Transfer mixture to processor and blend to thick but not smooth paste, about 10 seconds, stopping to scrape down sides of bowl. Mix in egg white, 1¹/₂ teaspoons lemon juice and maple extract using 2 on/off turns. Transfer to bowl. Cover and refrigerate. (*Can be prepared 2 days ahead.*)

To assemble: Divide dough in half. Wrap and refrigerate 1 half. Roll remainder out on floured cloth into 8 × 11-inch rectangle about ¹/₈ inch thick. Spread half of filling over dough. Starting from long edge, roll dough up into cylinder 1¹/₂ inches in diameter, using cloth as aid. Wrap cylinder in plastic. Repeat with remaining dough. Freeze until firm. (*Can be prepared 2 days ahead.*)

Position rack in center of oven and preheat to 350°F. Line jelly roll pans with foil. Lightly butter foil. Cut each cylinder into 24 slices. Arrange slices on prepared pans, spacing evenly. Bake until edges are lightly browned and bottoms are golden, about 25 minutes. Let stand 3 minutes on pans. Cool completely on rack. Store cookies in airtight container.

Fruit- and Chocolate-Filled Cookie Rolls (Cucidati)

A traditional Sicilian treat.

Makes about 3 dozen

Filling

2 ounces semisweet chocolate
2 ounces dried figs, stemmed and halved
2 ounces (scant 1/2 cup) raisins
2 ounces dried apricots, peaches, pears, apples or combination
1 1/2 ounces Glacéed Orange Peel (see recipe, page ••), coarsely chopped
1/4 cup honey
1/8 teaspoon ground allspice
1/8 teaspoon cinnamon

Pastry

1/4 cup (1/2 stick) butter, room temperature
1/4 cup sugar
1 egg
1 teaspoon grated lemon peel
1 1/4 cups all purpose flour
1 teaspoon baking powder

For filling: Coarsely chop chocolate in processor or food grinder. Add all dried fruit and orange peel and chop finely. Blend in honey and spices. Refrigerate in airtight container 2 hours. (*Can be stored up to 2 weeks.*)

For pastry: Cream butter and sugar with electric mixer. Beat in egg and lemon peel. Mix in flour and baking powder until smooth dough forms. Wrap with plastic. Cover and refrigerate at least 1 hour or overnight.

Preheat oven to 375°F. Divide pastry and filling into thirds. Roll one portion of pastry out on lightly floured surface to 3 × 13-inch strip. Trim edges. Form one portion of filling into 13-inch rope. Arrange atop pastry 1 inch from one long edge. Fold far edge of pastry over filling. Brush with water and fold up near edge to enclose filling. Pinch edges to seal. Cut pastry diagonally into 1-inch pieces. Arrange seam side down on ungreased baking sheets, spacing 1 inch apart. Repeat with remaining dough. Bake until cookies are golden, about 14 minutes. Cool completely on racks. Store cookies in airtight container.

Vanilla Crescents with Pistachio Filling

These cookies are best when served the same day as baked.

Makes 24

Vanilla Sugar

3/4 cup sugar
1 2-inch piece vanilla bean, split and diced

Filling

8 ounces raw pistachio nuts, shelled
1 egg white
1 drop of vanilla
1 drop of almond extract

Dough

1/2 cup (1 stick) well-chilled butter, cubed
1 1/4 cups sifted all purpose flour
1/3 cup sour cream
1 egg yolk

Glaze

1 egg yolk
1 teaspoon water

For vanilla sugar: Mix sugar and vanilla bean in processor 2 minutes, stopping every 30 seconds to scrape down sides of bowl. Spoon into jar; seal tightly. Let stand at least 1 day. (*Can be prepared up to 3 days ahead.*)

For filling: Blanch pistachios in rapidly boiling water 10 seconds. Remove with slotted spoon; drain on paper towels. Wrap in plastic. Refrigerate 3 hours.

Peel skin off pistachios. Sieve vanilla sugar through fine strainer. Mix pistachios, 2 tablespoons vanilla sugar, egg white, vanilla and almond extract in processor using on/off turns to almost smooth paste, stopping to scrape down sides of bowl. Scrape into bowl. Cover and refrigerate until ready to use. (*Can be prepared 2 days ahead.*)

For dough: Cut butter into flour in processor using 15 on/off turns. Add sour cream and yolk and blend using on/off turns until mixture forms moist beads. Turn out onto plastic wrap; flatten into disc. Wrap and refrigerate. (*Can be prepared 2 days ahead.*)

To assemble: Position rack in center of oven and preheat to 375°F. Line jelly roll pans with foil. Lightly butter foil. Divide dough in half. Wrap and refrigerate 1 half. Shape remainder into round. Sprinkle 1 tablespoon vanilla sugar onto work surface. Set dough atop sugar. Sprinkle 1 tablespoon vanilla sugar over dough. Roll dough out into 12-inch circle about 1/8 inch thick. Sprinkle top and bottom of dough with 2 tablespoons more vanilla sugar while rolling. Cut dough into 12 triangles using fluted pastry cutter. Shape half of filling into 12 ovals. Set 1 oval at base of each triangle. Roll triangles up from base to point to form cylinder. Arrange cylinders on prepared pan. Form into horseshoes (crescents will form while baking). Repeat with remaining dough. Bake 15 minutes. (To prevent bottoms of crescents from burning, set empty baking sheet on bottom shelf of oven during baking.)

Meanwhile, prepare glaze: Combine 1 tablespoon vanilla sugar, yolk and water in bowl and whisk to blend.

Brush glaze lightly over hot crescents. Continue baking until lightly browned, about 5 minutes. Slide foil onto rack and cool crescents 5 minutes. Set crescents on rack and cool.

Ruthie's Rugelach

These delicious cookies are a nice gift to take along when visiting friends. Don't hesitate to freeze them; just warm through before serving.

Makes about 64

3 cups all purpose flour
1 package dry yeast
1 cup (2 sticks) butter, cut into small pieces
3 egg yolks
1 cup sour cream

1 cup chopped walnuts
1 cup sugar
2 teaspoons cinnamon

Combine flour and yeast in large bowl. Cut in butter, mixing until dough is crumbly. Stir in egg yolks. Blend in sour cream. Flatten dough into disc. Cover with plastic wrap and refrigerate overnight.

Preheat oven to 350°F. Combine walnuts, sugar and cinnamon in medium bowl. Sprinkle 1/4 of mixture into 8-inch circle on work surface. Divide dough into 4 equal portions. Place one on top of nut mixture. Roll out into circle about 1/8 inch thick and 9 to 10 inches in diameter, lifting dough as you roll and pushing nut mixture back underneath. Cut circle into 16 wedges. Roll each triangle up from outside edge to point, then bend to form crescent. Transfer to lightweight aluminum baking sheet. Bake until puffed, golden and cooked through, about 15 to 20 minutes. Cool on rack. Repeat with remaining dough and nut mixture.

Sweet Ravioli (Ravioli Dolci)

A specialty of Liguria, the area around Genoa on Italy's northwest coast. Potato flour produces a very short, crisp cookie with a delicate crumb.

Makes about 3 dozen

½ cup (1 stick) unsalted butter, room temperature
½ cup sugar
1 egg
2 tablespoons brandy
1 teaspoon grated lemon peel
1 teaspoon vanilla

1¼ cups all purpose flour
1 cup potato flour*
⅛ teaspoon salt

**Thick apricot or cherry jam
Powdered sugar**

Cream butter and ½ cup sugar with electric mixer. Beat in egg, brandy, lemon peel and vanilla. Blend in both flours and salt. Refrigerate dough at least 2 hours or overnight.

Preheat oven to 350°F. Butter baking sheets. Roll half of dough out on generously floured surface into ⅛-inch-thick rectangle (keep remaining dough refrigerated). Using fluted pastry wheel guided with ruler, cut dough into 2-inch squares. Arrange on prepared sheets. Top each with ½ teaspoon jam, leaving ¼-inch border. Roll and cut remaining dough as above. Brush borders of jam-covered squares with water. Top each with second dough square, pressing edges to seal. Bake until cookies are beginning to brown, about 18 minutes. Cool completely on racks. Store in airtight container. Sift powdered sugar lightly over cookies before serving.

*Also called potato starch. Available at European markets and in kosher products section of most markets. Do not use the coarser flour sold at natural foods stores.

Hamantaschen

These traditional filled cookies are shaped like three-cornered hats.

Makes 4 dozen

1 cup vegetable oil
1 cup sugar
2 eggs
4 cups all purpose flour
½ cup fresh orange juice
2 teaspoons baking powder

1 teaspoon vanilla
½ teaspoon salt
1½ 12-ounce cans poppy seed, prune or apricot filling

Preheat oven to 350°F. Grease baking sheets. Beat oil, sugar and eggs in large bowl of electric mixer. Stir in flour, orange juice, baking powder, vanilla and salt. Roll dough out on floured surface to thickness of ⅛ to ¼ inch. Cut into 3½-inch circles using glass. Place 1 heaping teaspoon filling in center of each. Fold edges into center to form triangle-shaped cookie. Pinch corners to seal. Transfer to prepared baking sheets. Bake until golden, 15 to 20 minutes. Cool completely. Store in airtight container.

Almond Butterballs with Tart Apricot Filling

Makes 36

Dough
- 1 cup blanched almonds, toasted and cooled
- 1/2 cup superfine sugar
- 1 1/2 cups sifted all purpose flour
- 1 teaspoon finely grated lemon peel
- 1/4 teaspoon salt
- 1/4 teaspoon baking powder
- 3/4 cup (1 1/2 sticks) well-chilled unsalted butter, cubed
- 2 tablespoons beaten egg
- 1 teaspoon vanilla
- 1 teaspoon almond extract

Filling
- 5 tablespoons apricot preserves
- 2 teaspoons orange liqueur
- 1 teaspoon fresh lemon juice
- 1/4 teaspoon vanilla
- 6 ounces dried apricots, finely chopped

Glaze
- 1 cup powdered sugar
- 2 tablespoons plus 1 teaspoon amaretto liqueur
- 1 teaspoon milk

For dough: Finely chop almonds with sugar in processor. Transfer to large bowl. Combine flour, lemon peel, salt and baking powder in processor. Mix in butter until coarse meal forms. Blend in egg, vanilla and almond extract until mixture holds together. Knead into almond mixture. Turn dough out onto 15-inch piece of plastic wrap. Shape dough into 9 × 2-inch cylinder. Wrap and refrigerate for 2 hours. (*Can be prepared 2 days ahead.*)

For filling: Blend preserves, liqueur, lemon juice and vanilla in small bowl. Stir in apricots. Cover and refrigerate. (*Can be prepared 2 days ahead.*)

To assemble: Cut cylinder into 36 slices. Bring slices to room temperature. Line baking sheets with foil. Butter and flour foil, shaking off excess. Set 1 dough slice on 10- to 12-inch piece of plastic wrap. Using fingertips, press down into 3-inch round. Spoon 1 teaspoon filling into center of round. Place plastic-lined round in cupped hand. Using plastic as aid, close dough over filling, twisting plastic tightly to seal. Carefully remove plastic. Roll between hands to form round. Set round seam side down on prepared sheet. Repeat with remaining dough and filling. Cover and refrigerate 30 minutes.

Position rack in center of oven and preheat to 350°F. Bake cookies until lightly colored and bottoms are browned, about 20 minutes. Cool cookies completely on rack.

For glaze: Blend all ingredients until smooth. Dip tops of cookies into glaze. Arrange on rack over waxed paper. Let stand until glaze is firm. (*Can be prepared 1 day ahead. Store loosely covered at room temperature.*)

Special Florentines

Coconut is a crunchy addition to this classic cookie, updated in looks by being "sandwiched" with a delectable double chocolate filling.

Makes about 24

- 1 cup (2 sticks) unsalted butter
- 8 ounces ground pecans (about 2 cups)
- 2/3 cup sugar
- 2/3 cup flaked coconut
- 2 tablespoons milk
- 2 tablespoons all purpose flour
- 2 teaspoons vanilla

- 12 ounces semisweet chocolate, coarsely chopped
- 2 ounces unsweetened chocolate, coarsely chopped

Preheat oven to 350°F. Line baking sheet with foil. Line work surface with waxed paper. Melt butter in heavy medium saucepan over low heat. Remove from heat. Add remaining ingredients except chocolate and stir well. Drop batter by rounded teaspoonfuls onto prepared sheet, spacing 4 inches apart (about 5 cookies per sheet). Keep remaining batter warm over very low heat. Bake cookies 10 minutes. Slip foil off sheet. Let cookies cool until firm, about 10 minutes. Using thin spatula, transfer cookies to waxed paper. Repeat with remaining cookie batter, stirring well before using.

Melt chocolates in double boiler over gently simmering water; stir until smooth. Take 2 cookies of similar size. Spread bottom of 1 cookie with 1 teaspoon melted chocolate. Top chocolate with second cookie, pressing gently to form "sandwich." Repeat with remaining cookies. Let cool. (*Can be prepared 1 month ahead and frozen. Store between layers of waxed paper. Bring to room temperature before serving.*)

Chocolate-Dipped Sandwich Wafers

These dainty cookies will keep up to two weeks in an airtight container.

Makes about 64

Butter
Flour
3/4 cup (1½ sticks) unsalted butter, room temperature
3/4 cup sugar
Pinch of salt
4 egg whites, room temperature
1 teaspoon vanilla
1½ cups sifted all purpose flour

8 ounces bittersweet or semisweet chocolate, coarsely chopped
1 ounce unsweetened chocolate, coarsely chopped
1 tablespoon solid vegetable shortening

Position rack in center of oven and preheat to 400°F. Butter and flour 2 baking sheets. Cream 3/4 cup butter until fluffy, using electric mixer. Slowly add sugar and beat until mixture is very fluffy. Add salt. Beat in whites 1 at a time and continue beating until mixture is creamy. If mixture begins to curdle, increase speed and beat until smooth. Add vanilla. Using spatula, gently fold in flour.

Place batter in pastry bag fitted with 1/4-inch plain tip. Pipe mixture onto prepared sheets in ½ × 2½-inch "fingers," spacing about 3/4 inch apart. (Batter can also be spread with spoon.) Flatten any points with back of spoon dipped in water. Bake 1 sheet until cookie edges are golden brown and centers firm, about 12 minutes. Transfer to rack. Repeat with second sheet. Cool cookies to room temperature.

Line baking sheet with waxed paper. Melt chocolates and shortening in double boiler over barely simmering water. Stir until smooth. Spread chocolate in thin layer on bottom of 1 cookie. Place another cookie over chocolate, flat side in. Set on prepared sheet. Repeat with remaining cookies. Refrigerate until chocolate is solid.

Reheat remaining chocolate over barely simmering water. Remove from heat. Dip tips of cookies in chocolate and return to sheet. Refrigerate until chocolate is firm, about 20 minutes. Serve at room temperature.

Oak Leaf Tortes

Beautiful cookie tortes for a special occasion.

8 servings

Oak Leaves
2/3 cup blanched whole almonds
1 cup sugar
2 cups sifted cake flour
5 eggs, beaten to blend
1/2 cup (1 stick) unsalted butter, melted and cooled
1/2 teaspoon almond extract

Almond Buttercream
1 cup blanched whole almonds
1 2/3 cups powdered sugar

1 cup (2 sticks) well-chilled unsalted butter, quartered
4 egg yolks
1 teaspoon almond extract

Powdered sugar

For leaves: Preheat oven to 350°F. Finely chop almonds in processor. Add sugar and process until almonds are pulverized, about 10 seconds. Add flour and mix 5 seconds. Pour eggs in circle over dry ingredients. Repeat with butter. Add almond extract. Process using on/off turns until batter is just mixed, stopping once to scrape down sides of work bowl.

Place 4 1/2-inch-long oak leaf stencil* on nonstick baking sheet or baking sheet lined with parchment. Spread 1 teaspoon batter evenly in stencil, using flexible spatula. Clean excess batter off top of stencil, using spatula. Lift stencil straight up (if using parchment paper, hold down to prevent batter from smearing). Repeat, spacing "leaves" 1 inch apart. Bake until light brown, 8 to 9 minutes. Transfer to rack, using spatula. Let cool. Repeat with remaining batter. If necessary, maintain consistency of batter by adding water 1/2 teaspoon at a time. (*Can be prepared up to 1 week ahead. Store cookies in airtight container.*)

For buttercream: Finely chop almonds in processor, about 30 seconds. Add 1 2/3 cups powdered sugar. Blend until nuts are pulverized. Arrange butter in circle atop almonds. Process until ball forms. Flatten mixture evenly around blade, using spatula. Arrange yolks in circle atop nut mixture. Add extract. Mix until well blended, stopping once to scrap down sides of work bowl, about 15 seconds. (*Can be prepared 3 days ahead and refrigerated. Bring to room temperature before continuing.*)

Divide leaves evenly into 8 stacks. Spread 1 teaspoon buttercream lengthwise down center of 1 leaf. Top with another leaf, pressing gently together. Repeat until 1 stack is assembled. Starting at bottom of stack, gently press base of leaves together at intervals of every 4 leaves to fan upper end of stack. Repeat with remaining buttercream and leaves.

Cover half of one top leaf with cardboard. Sieve powdered sugar over half of leaf. Repeat with remaining stacks. (*Can be prepared 6 hours ahead.*) Arrange tortes on platter and serve.

*Available at specialty cookware stores.

Kransekake (Crown Cake)

Decorate this spectacular "cookie tree" in the traditional style with white icing, or tint some of it red and some green for a festive holiday look. Guests can break off pieces to enjoy with coffee or tea.

Makes one 15- to 20-inch cookie tree

1 **pound almonds (skins intact)**
1 **pound powdered sugar**
2 **eggs**

Sugar Icing*

Preheat oven to 350°F. Cut 8 pieces of parchment paper to fit baking sheet. Finely grind almonds ½ cup at a time with 2 heaping tablespoons powdered sugar for each batch in processor or blender. Transfer to large bowl and add remaining powdered sugar. Mix in eggs. Blend until dough is sticky and ingredients are incorporated.

Using pencil, draw about 20 circles on parchment paper starting with circle 1 inch in diameter and increasing diameters by ¼ inch. Allow 2 inches between each circle.

Place heavy cloth on work surface. Roll dough into ropes ½ inch thick and as long as necessary to outline border of each circle. Place parchment pieces with largest circles on 2 baking sheets. Carefully arrange ropes on patterns. Firmly pinch ends together to close rings. Cover remaining dough and set aside. Bake rings until lightly browned, about 10 minutes. (Rings will expand.) Carefully slide paper with rings off baking sheets. Repeat with remaining patterns and dough ropes. Cool rings on paper.

Spoon icing into pastry bag fitted with ⅛-inch plain tip. Remove rings from paper and stack on large serving platter, beginning with largest ring on bottom and piping icing between each layer while assembling. Decorate tree with remaining icing.

*Sugar Icing

Makes about 1⅓ cups

3¼ **cups powdered sugar**
2 **egg whites**

¼ **teaspoon distilled white vinegar**
1 **tablespoon hot water (optional)**

Mix powdered sugar, whites, and vinegar in small bowl of electric mixer until smooth; consistency should be thick enough to hold shape when piped. Add hot water 1 drop at a time, mixing well after each addition, if icing is too thick for piping on Kransekake.

5 ❦ Bar Cookies

Crisp on the outside, moist and chewy on the inside, bar cookies are absolutely the quickest and easiest to prepare. No special handling of the batter or dough is required, other than spreading it evenly into a prepared pan. After baking, the cookie "cake" is cut into bars or squares. The only difficult thing here, in fact, is keeping them from being eaten up the minute they're done.

Bar cookies come in a delicious variety of flavors and colors, from fruit-filled Apricot Bars (page 78) and Cherry Chews (page 81) to nutty Pecan Diamonds (page 87) and Walnut Dreams (page 87).

Brownies are a particular favorite in this category. You'll find the perfect ratio of chocolate to nuts in classic Chocolate Nut Brownies (page 93), as well as imaginative variations such as Brownies with Peanut Butter and Caramel Filling (page 95) and Hazelnut Chocolate Chunk Brownies (page 94).

Shortbread, basically a very simple combination of ingredients—butter chief among them—has its own loyal followers. Try the traditional Scotch Shortbread (page 97), to fancier versions such as Apricot-Filled Italian Shortbread (page 99), Raisin Shortbread (page 98) and Millionaire's Shortbread (page 99), topped with chewy caramel and chocolate.

To ensure that they have that perfect crispy-chewy consistency, be sure to bake bar cookies in the pan that is called for in the recipe. If you decide to substitute a different size, remember that a larger pan will yield thinner bars and require less baking time; a smaller one will yield a thicker result that will need longer baking time. But thick or thin, you will find that these bar cookies taste just right every time.

Oatmeal Brownies

These "brownies," popular in Scotland, are actually crisp biscuits.

Makes about 4 dozen

1 cup (2 sticks) unsalted butter, melted
1 cup firmly packed brown sugar
6 cups quick-cooking oats

½ cup all purpose flour
2 teaspoons baking soda
2 teaspoons cinnamon

Preheat oven to 350°F. Lightly grease 13 × 9-inch jelly roll pan. Mix butter and sugar in medium bowl. Stir in oats. Combine flour, baking soda and cinnamon; gently mix into oats. Press firmly and evenly into prepared pan. Roll over top with rolling pin to smooth. Bake 15 minutes. Reduce temperature to 300°F. Continue baking until edges are golden brown, 25 to 30 minutes. Cut into 1½-inch squares while hot. Cool completely in pan on rack. Store cookies in airtight container.

Scottish Butter Cookies

Makes about 4 dozen

1 cup (2 sticks) unsalted butter, room temperature
⅔ cup sugar
2 cups all purpose flour

2 teaspoons vanilla
¼ teaspoon salt
Powdered sugar

Preheat oven to 350°F. Cream butter with sugar in large bowl until smooth. Gradually blend in flour, vanilla and salt and mix thoroughly. Pat mixture evenly into ungreased 10 × 15-inch jelly roll pan. Sprinkle top with powdered sugar. Bake until golden, about 16 to 18 minutes. Cool 5 minutes, then cut into squares while still warm. Store cookies in airtight container.

Apricot Bars

Makes about 5 dozen bars

1 cup dried apricots

½ cup (1 stick) unsalted butter, room temperature
2 cups firmly packed light brown sugar
2 eggs
1 tablespoon apricot brandy, brandy or whiskey
1 teaspoon grated fresh orange peel
1½ cups unbleached all purpose flour
1 teaspoon baking powder
½ teaspoon salt

Icing
1 cup sifted powdered sugar
2 teaspoons fresh orange juice
2 teaspoons fresh lemon juice
2 teaspoons butter, room temperature
1 teaspoon grated fresh orange peel

½ cup finely ground walnuts

Grease 10 × 15-inch jelly roll pan. Place apricots in medium bowl and cover with boiling water. Let soak 10 to 15 minutes. Drain well. Cut apricots into small bite-size pieces. Set aside.

Preheat oven to 350°F. Cream butter with sugar in large bowl until light and fluffy. Add eggs, brandy and orange peel and mix thoroughly. Blend in flour, baking powder and salt. Fold in apricots. Turn mixture into prepared pan, spreading evenly. Bake until tester inserted in center comes out clean, about 25 to 30 minutes.

Meanwhile, prepare icing. Blend powdered sugar, orange and lemon juices, butter and orange peel in small bowl until smooth and creamy.

Remove pan from oven and let cool on wire rack 10 minutes. Cover evenly with icing. Sprinkle with nuts, pressing lightly. Cool completely before slicing. Store in airtight container.

Apricot-Oatmeal Bars

Makes 24

3 cups dried apricots
3 cups water
1/2 cup sugar

2 cups all purpose flour
1³/4 cups rolled oats

1 cup firmly packed brown sugar
3/4 cup (1¹/2 sticks) butter, melted
1/4 cup wheat germ
1 teaspoon baking soda
1 teaspoon vanilla

Combine first 3 ingredients in medium saucepan over medium-high heat. Stir until sugar dissolves, about 5 minutes. Reduce heat and simmer until almost all water is absorbed, about 15 minutes. Remove from heat. Mash apricots.

Preheat oven to 350°F. Combine remaining ingredients in large bowl and mix well. Press half of crumb mixture into bottom of 9 × 13-inch baking pan. Spread evenly with apricot filling. Top with remaining crumb mixture, pressing down lightly to flatten. Bake until lightly browned, 30 to 35 minutes. Cool in pan. Cut into bars.

Apricot-Oat Squares

Makes 25 to 30

2 cups quick-cooking oats
1³/4 cups all purpose flour
1 cup (2 sticks) margarine, room
temperature
3/4 cup firmly packed brown sugar

1¹/2 teaspoons cinnamon
1/2 teaspoon baking soda
1 cup apricot preserves

Preheat oven to 400°F. Butter 9 × 13-inch baking pan. Mix first 6 ingredients in large bowl until crumbly. Set 2 cups oat mixture aside. Press remainder into bottom of prepared pan. Spread preserves over. Crumble reserved oat mixture over apricot preserves. Bake until golden brown, about 20 minutes. Cut into squares and serve.

Apricot-Date Bars

*Make this quick treat in
the microwave.*

Makes 20 to 24 bars

1/2 cup pitted dates, coarsely
chopped
Flour
1 cup apricot jam
1/2 cup (1 stick) butter
1 cup firmly packed brown sugar
2 eggs
1³/4 cups all purpose flour
1 teaspoon baking soda
1 teaspoon vanilla

1 teaspoon salt
1 cup walnuts, coarsely chopped
1/2 cup finely chopped walnuts
(garnish)

Grease bottom of 10-inch microwave-safe quiche dish. Dredge dates in flour, shaking off excess. Transfer to small bowl and add jam. Cream butter with sugar in processor or large bowl of electric mixer. Add eggs one at a time, beating well after each addition. Add flour, baking soda, vanilla and salt and mix well. Stir in 1 cup coarsely chopped walnuts. Spread 2/3 of dough into bottom of prepared dish. Top with all of date mixture. Drop remaining dough over dates by spoonfuls. Sprinkle with 1/2 cup finely chopped walnuts. Cook on Medium-High (70 percent power) 11 to 12 minutes (do not overcook). Let stand 10 minutes. Cut into bars and serve.

Lemon Squares

Makes about 2 dozen

2 cups all purpose flour
1/2 cup sugar
1 cup (2 sticks) butter, well chilled

4 eggs
2 cups sugar

1/4 cup all purpose flour
1 teaspoon baking powder
6 tablespoons fresh lemon juice

Preheat oven to 350°F. Combine 2 cups flour and 1/2 cup sugar in medium bowl. Cut in butter using pastry blender or 2 knives until consistency of coarse meal. Press dough into bottom of 9 × 13-inch baking dish. Bake crust until golden, about 20 minutes.

Meanwhile, beat eggs in large bowl of electric mixer on medium speed. Gradually add 2 cups sugar, beating constantly. Mix in 1/4 cup flour and baking powder. Add lemon juice and blend well. Pour into crust, spreading evenly. Bake until set, about 25 minutes. Cool in pan on rack. Cut into squares. Store in airtight container.

Blueberry Bublanina

In Czechoslovakia, this is served as either a dessert or as a morning sweet.

8 to 10 servings

Butter
1/2 cup (1 stick) unsalted butter, room temperature
1/2 cup sugar
3 egg yolks, room temperature
1 tablespoon Grand Marnier or other orange liqueur
1 teaspoon grated orange peel
1/2 teaspoon salt

2 egg whites, room temperature
Pinch of cream of tartar
1 cup all purpose flour
2 cups fresh or frozen (unthawed) blueberries
Powdered sugar

Position rack in center of oven and preheat to 350°F. Butter 8 × 10-inch baking pan. Using electric mixer, cream 1/2 cup butter, sugar and yolks in large bowl until light and fluffy. Blend in Grand Marnier, orange peel and salt. Beat whites with cream of tartar in another bowl until stiff but not dry. Fold whites into batter alternately with flour. Turn batter into prepared pan, smoothing top. Cover with blueberries, pressing gently into batter with spatula or spoon. Bake until cake is springy to touch, 42 to 47 minutes. (*Can be prepared 1 day ahead. Cool and wrap tightly. Rewarm in 350°F oven 5 minutes.*) Cut cake into 2-inch squares. Dust top lightly with powdered sugar. Serve warm.

Cherry Chews

Makes about 6 dozen

6 ounces egg whites (about 3 large),
  at room temperature
1/4 teaspoon salt
1 3/4 cups sugar

6 ounces (about 2 cups) chopped
  pecans

6 ounces chopped glacéed cherries
5 ounces (1 1/4 sticks) butter, melted
1 1/2 teaspoons vanilla
1 3/4 cups sifted cake flour

Preheat oven to 350°F. Line 9 × 13-inch baking pan with buttered waxed paper. Beat egg whites with salt until foamy. Gradually add sugar and beat until stiff.

    Combine pecans, cherries, butter and vanilla. Fold into whites alternately with flour. Spread into baking pan and bake until dry, about 45 minutes. Let cool before cutting Cherry Chews into squares.

Coconut Custard Bars

Makes about 50

Cookie Crust
3 ounces fresh coconut, peeled and
  cut into 1 1/2-inch squares
  Butter

1 3-inch piece vanilla bean, cut into
  1-inch lengths
1 cup sugar
1 cup (2 sticks) unsalted butter, cut
  into 8 pieces, room temperature
1 egg yolk

1/8 teaspoon salt
2 cups unbleached all purpose flour

Custard
1 1-inch piece vanilla bean
1/2 cup sugar
2 eggs
  Pinch of salt
1/3 cup whipping cream

For crust: Position rack in center of oven and preheat to 325°F.

    Place coconut in processor feed tube and shred using firm pressure. Spread in 10 1/2 × 15 1/2-inch jelly roll pan. Bake until light brown, stirring occasionally, about 15 minutes. Transfer to small bowl and set aside. Reduce oven temperature to 300°F. Cool pan slightly and coat with butter.

    Using steel knife, finely grind vanilla bean in processor with 1/2 cup sugar, about 3 minutes. Add remaining 1/2 cup sugar, 1 cup butter, yolk and salt and blend until fluffy, about 30 seconds, stopping once to scrape down sides of work bowl. Reserve 3 tablespoons coconut for topping; add remaining coconut and flour to work bowl and mix until just combined, using on/off turns. Spread dough in prepared pan, smoothing with hand (cover hand with plastic bag to prevent sticking). Bake until light brown, about 45 minutes. Cool completely.

    For custard: Position rack in center of oven and preheat to 325°F.

    Finely grind vanilla bean with sugar in processor, about 2 minutes. Add eggs and salt and blend 30 seconds, stopping once to scrape down sides of work bowl. Add cream and mix 5 seconds. Spread custard evenly over cooled crust. Sprinkle with reserved coconut. Bake until custard is set, about 15 minutes. Cool completely. Cut into bars.

Coconut Squares

For two different flavors, spread half the pastry with apricot-pineapple jam and half with currant jelly.

Makes about 12 dozen

Coconut Topping
- ³/₄ cup (1¹/₂ sticks) unsalted butter
- ¹/₃ cup sugar
- 3 tablespoons water
- 1 14-ounce package sweetened flaked coconut
- ¹/₂ teaspoon vanilla

Pastry
- 2 cups sifted all purpose flour
- 1 cup (2 sticks) well-chilled unsalted butter, cut into tablespoons

- ¹/₂ cup sugar
- 2 egg yolks
- ¹/₂ teaspoon vanilla

- ²/₃ cup apricot-pineapple jam or currant jelly

For topping: Combine butter, sugar and water in heavy saucepan and boil, stirring occasionally, until butter melts. Mix in coconut and vanilla. Cool.

For pastry: Position rack in lower third of oven and preheat to 350°F. Butter 10 × 15-inch jelly roll pan. Place flour in processor. Arrange butter in circle atop flour. Process until butter is incorporated, stopping once to scrape down sides of work bowl. Add sugar and mix 5 seconds. Add yolks and vanilla. Blend until ball forms, about 20 seconds. Redistribute dough if necessary and process for 5 seconds to knead.

Roll dough out between sheets of waxed paper to 10 × 15-inch rectangle. Transfer to prepared pan, discarding paper. Bake until beginning to color, about 15 minutes. Cool 10 minutes. Retain oven at 350°F.

Spread jam over pastry. Spread topping over jam. Position rack in center of oven. Bake pastry until topping is light brown and bubbly, about 20 minutes. Cool completely. Cut into 1-inch squares before serving.

Raspberry-Almond Squares

Makes 54 1¹/₂-inch squares

- ²/₃ cup blanched whole almonds (4 ounces)
- 2 cups unbleached all purpose flour
- ³/₄ teaspoon cinnamon
- ¹/₄ teaspoon salt
- 1 egg, separated

- 1 cup sugar
- ¹/₄ cup lightly packed light brown sugar

- 1 teaspoon vanilla
- 1 cup (2 sticks) unsalted butter, cut into 8 pieces, room temperature

- ²/₃ cup raspberry preserves

Lightly butter 11 × 14-inch jelly roll pan. Position rack in center of oven and preheat to 350°F.

Mince nuts in processor using 8 on/off turns, then mix until nuts are finely chopped *but not powdered*. Remove and set aside. Add flour, cinnamon and salt to work bowl and mix 2 seconds. Remove and set aside. Mix egg white in work bowl 5 seconds. Transfer to small bowl.

Combine sugars, vanilla and egg yolk in work bowl and mix 1 minute. Add butter and blend 1 minute. Add flour and combine using 5 on/off turns.

Using waxed paper as aid, press dough into prepared pan. Spread preserves evenly over top. Brush reserved egg white lightly over preserves. Sprinkle with nuts, pressing gently. Bake until edges are brown and center is almost firm, about 30 to 35 minutes. Remove from oven and immediately loosen sides with spatula. Let cool in pan 40 minutes, then cut into squares.

Persimmon Bars

These bars stay fresh two to three days in an airtight container.

Makes thirty 3 × 1¹/₂-inch bars

1 cup fresh persimmon puree (about 3 large persimmons)
1¹/₂ teaspoons fresh lemon juice
1 teaspoon baking soda
1 egg
1 cup sugar
1 cup (6 ounces) pitted dates, finely snipped

¹/₂ cup safflower oil
1³/₄ cups all purpose flour
1 teaspoon cinnamon
1 teaspoon freshly grated nutmeg
¹/₄ teaspoon ground cloves
1 cup (4 ounces) walnuts, chopped
Powdered sugar

Preheat oven to 350°F. Butter and flour 10 × 15-inch jelly roll pan. Blend persimmon puree with lemon juice and baking soda in medium bowl. Beat egg to blend in large bowl. Stir in sugar, dates and safflower oil. Blend flour and spices. Stir into date mixture alternately with persimmon puree; do not overmix. Fold in nuts. Spread evenly in prepared pan. Bake until lightly browned, about 25 minutes. Cool in pan on rack 5 minutes. Dust with sugar. Cool completely. Cut into bars. Store in airtight container.

Pineapple Scotchies

Makes 12 to 16 bars

1¹/₂ cups all purpose flour
1¹/₂ cups quick-cooking oats
1 cup firmly packed light brown sugar
³/₄ cup (1¹/₂ sticks) butter or margarine

¹/₂ teaspoon baking soda
1 16-ounce can crushed pineapple, drained
¹/₄ cup sugar
3 tablespoons apricot or grape jam

Grease 9-inch square ovenproof glass baking dish. Combine flour, oats, brown sugar, butter and baking soda in processor and mix until crumbly using on/off turns (or mix using pastry blender or fork). Combine pineapple, sugar and jam in medium saucepan. Bring to boil over medium heat, stirring. Let cool.

Preheat oven to 375°F. Sprinkle half of flour mixture in prepared dish. Top with pineapple filling. Spread remaining flour mixture over pineapple. Pat down gently. Bake until golden brown, 35 to 40 minutes. Cool to room temperature. Cover Scotchies with plastic wrap and let stand at room temperature overnight. Cut into bars to serve.

Currant Bars

Makes 24 to 28 bars

Pastry
1/2 cup (1 stick) butter, room
  temperature
1/4 cup sugar
1 egg yolk

2 cups all purpose flour
1 teaspoon baking powder
1 teaspoon cornstarch
1 teaspoon vanilla
3 tablespoons water (about)

Filling
1 cup dried currants
1/2 cup currant jelly
2 tablespoons cassis syrup

2 tablespoons all purpose flour
1 egg white
1 tablespoon water
Powdered sugar

For pastry: Combine butter and sugar in large mixing bowl and beat until light and fluffy. Add egg yolk and continue beating until well blended. Slowly stir in 2 cups flour with baking powder and cornstarch, mixing well. Add vanilla and enough water to make dough pliable. Chill 30 minutes. (*Pastry can be prepared ahead and frozen.*)

For filling: Combine currants, jelly and cassis syrup in small saucepan and soften over low heat. Remove from heat.

Position rack in center of oven and preheat to 375°F. Lightly oil baking sheet and set aside. Divide dough into 4 equal parts and roll into cylinders. Flour 16-inch sheet of waxed paper. Place 1 pastry cylinder on paper and roll into 10 × 4-inch rectangle 1/4 inch thick. Trim edges. Repeat with 3 more sheets of waxed paper and 3 cylinders.

Blend 2 tablespoons flour into filling. Spoon 1/4 of filling down center of each rectangle. Fold each long side of rectangles over to meet in center. Combine egg white and 1 tablespoon water in small mixing bowl. Brush each rectangle with egg wash. Cut each into 6 to 7 pieces, depending on size desired. Arrange bars on prepared baking sheet. Bake 18 to 20 minutes. Let cool completely. Dust with powdered sugar. (*Can be prepared ahead, wrapped tightly and frozen.*)

Butter Tart Squares

Makes about 25 to 30 squares

1/2 cup (1 stick) butter, cut into
  pieces
1 cup sifted all purpose flour
2 tablespoons sugar

1 1/2 cups firmly packed brown sugar
2 eggs
2 tablespoons all purpose flour

1 teaspoon vanilla
1/2 teaspoon baking powder
1 cup plumped raisins
1/4 cup chopped walnuts (optional)

Preheat oven to 350°F. Cream butter in medium bowl until smooth. Add 1 cup flour with sugar and blend until flour is incorporated and mixture is smooth. Transfer to 9-inch square baking dish, spreading evenly. Bake until lightly brown, about 15 minutes. Set baking dish aside. (Retain oven temperature at 350°F.)

Combine brown sugar, eggs, remaining flour, vanilla and baking powder in large bowl and mix thoroughly. Stir in raisins and walnuts. Spread evenly over crust. Bake until golden, about 30 minutes. Let pastry cool completely before cutting into squares.

Eyemouth Tart

A rectangular tart from Eyemouth, Scotland, cut into bars for serving.

Makes about 4 dozen

Butter Pastry
2 cups all purpose flour
1/2 teaspoon salt
1 cup (2 sticks) unsalted butter
1 egg
2 to 3 tablespoons cold water
2 teaspoons fresh lemon juice

Fruit and Nut Filling
1 cup chopped walnuts
1 cup dried currants
1 cup flaked coconut

1 cup candied cherries, chopped
1 cup golden raisins
1 cup sugar
1/2 cup (1 stick) unsalted butter, melted and cooled
2 eggs, beaten to blend

Icing
2 cups powdered sugar, sifted
1/4 cup fresh orange juice

For pastry: Combine flour and salt in medium bowl. Cut in butter until coarse meal forms. Blend egg, 2 tablespoons water and lemon juice in small bowl. Slowly add to flour mixture, tossing with fork just until pastry holds together and adding remaining 1 tablespoon water if necessary. Wrap in plastic and refrigerate 30 minutes.

Preheat oven to 375°F. Roll pastry out between sheets of lightly floured waxed paper to 12 × 17-inch rectangle. Transfer to 10 × 15-inch jelly roll pan, removing paper. Crimp edges.

For filling: Combine first 6 ingredients in bowl. Mix in butter and eggs. Spread filling in pastry. Bake until firm to touch, about 30 minutes.

For icing: Mix sugar and orange juice in small bowl until smooth. Drizzle icing over hot tart. Cool completely. Cover and refrigerate overnight. Cut into 1 1/2 × 2-inch bars. (*Can be prepared 5 days ahead and refrigerated or up to 2 months ahead and frozen.*) Serve bars at room temperature.

Almond Cookies

Makes about 4 dozen

1 cup (2 sticks) butter, room temperature
1 scant cup sugar
1 egg, separated

1 teaspoon vanilla
2 cups sifted all purpose flour
Cinnamon
2 ounces slivered almonds

Preheat oven to 300°F. Cream butter with sugar in large bowl. Add yolk and mix well. Blend in vanilla. Add flour and cinnamon and stir until smooth. Transfer dough to 11 × 15-inch baking sheet, spreading evenly to edges. Whisk egg white until foamy. Brush over dough. Sprinkle with almonds. Bake until top is golden and tester inserted in center comes out clean, about 45 to 50 minutes. Cut into bars while still hot. Let cool completely.

Pecan Bars

Serve these sweets with afternoon tea.

Makes 24

Crust
1¼ cups all purpose flour
⅓ cup sugar
½ cup (1 stick) butter, room temperature

Topping
½ cup firmly packed light brown sugar

2 eggs, beaten to blend
2 tablespoons all purpose flour
1 teaspoon vanilla
½ teaspoon baking powder
¼ teaspoon salt
1½ cups grated coconut
1 cup chopped pecans

For crust: Preheat oven to 375°F. Grease 9 × 12-inch baking pan. Mix flour and sugar in large bowl. Cut in butter until mixture resembles coarse meal. Gather into ball. Press into bottom of prepared pan. Bake until crust is golden brown, 10 to 15 minutes. Reduce oven temperature to 350°F.

For topping: Whisk first 6 ingredients in large bowl until smooth. Fold in coconut and pecans. Spread over crust. Bake until set, 20 to 25 minutes. Cut into 24 squares while still warm. Serve Pecan Bars warm or at room temperature.

Butter Pecan Squares

Makes about 2 dozen

Crust
1¼ cups all purpose flour
½ cup (1 stick) unsalted butter, room temperature
⅓ cup sugar

Filling
⅔ cup sugar
½ cup honey

2 eggs, beaten to blend
2 tablespoons (¼ stick) unsalted butter, melted
2 tablespoons all purpose flour
1½ teaspoons vanilla
1 teaspoon fresh lemon juice
¼ teaspoon salt
1 cup pecan halves

For crust: Preheat oven to 375°F. Combine all ingredients in small bowl of electric mixer and beat on low speed, scraping down sides of bowl frequently, just until mixture resembles coarse meal. Press dough evenly into bottom of 8- or 9-inch square baking dish. Bake until edges are lightly browned, 10 to 15 minutes. (Retain oven at 375°F.)

For filling: Combine sugar, honey, eggs, butter, flour, vanilla, lemon juice and salt in small bowl of electric mixer and beat on low speed until well blended, 1 to 2 minutes. Pour over crust. Arrange pecan halves atop filling. Bake until filling is set and crust is golden brown, 15 to 20 minutes. Cool completely. Cut into 1½-inch squares and serve.

Pecan Diamonds

These delectable confections are a specialty at New York's Windows on the World.

Makes about 75

Cookie Crust
3/4 cup (1 1/2 sticks) unsalted butter, room temperature
1/2 cup sugar
1 egg
2 1/4 cups unbleached all purpose flour

Pecan Filling
1 1/2 cups firmly packed light brown sugar

1 cup (2 sticks) unsalted butter
1/2 cup honey
1 pound pecans
1/4 cup whipping cream

For crust: Using electric mixer, cream butter and sugar until light and fluffy. Add egg and beat until fluffy. Add flour and mix until just combined. Gather dough into ball; flatten to rectangle. Cover and chill 30 minutes.

Line 9 × 13-inch baking pan with parchment. Roll dough out between sheets of waxed paper to 1/4-inch-thick rectangle. Transfer to prepared pan, discarding waxed paper. Trim edges. Refrigerate while preparing filling.

For filling: Preheat oven to 375°F. Heat sugar, butter and honey in heavy medium saucepan over low heat, swirling pan occasionally, until butter melts and sugar dissolves. Increase heat and bring to boil. Blend in pecans and cream; mixture will bubble.

Immediately spread pecan mixture over pastry. Bake until filling bubbles and is deep golden brown, about 25 minutes. Run knife between crust and pan. Cool completely. Invert pastry onto another baking pan, then invert onto work surface. Cut into 1 1/2-inch diamonds. Store in airtight container.

Walnut Dreams

Makes about 18 dozen 1-inch squares

1 cup (2 sticks) butter, room temperature
1/2 cup sugar
2 cups all purpose flour

1 pound brown sugar
2 cups chopped walnuts
1/4 cup all purpose flour
4 eggs
1 teaspoon salt

1 teaspoon baking powder
1 teaspoon vanilla

2 cups powdered sugar
3 tablespoons milk
2 tablespoons (1/4 stick) butter, melted
Almond extract

Preheat oven to 350°F. Grease 12 × 18-inch jelly roll pan. Cream 1 cup butter with 1/2 cup sugar in mixing bowl. Gradually add flour, blending well after each addition. Spread evenly in prepared pan and bake for 15 minutes.

Meanwhile, combine next 7 ingredients and blend well. Pour over crust. Continue baking until set, about 15 to 17 minutes. Let cool completely.

Combine remaining ingredients and blend until smooth. Spread evenly over pastry. Cut into squares before serving.

Sunflower-Rye Bars

These light and crunchy bars are great with afternoon coffee or tea, or with fresh fruit for dessert.

Makes about 15 bars

¹/₂ cup rye flour
¹/₂ cup quick-cooking oats
¹/₂ cup chopped walnuts
¹/₄ cup sunflower seeds
¹/₂ teaspoon baking powder
¹/₂ teaspoon salt

2 eggs
1 cup firmly packed dark brown sugar
¹/₃ cup vegetable oil
1 teaspoon vanilla

Preheat oven to 350°F. Grease bottom of 8-inch square baking pan. Combine flour, oats, walnuts, sunflower seeds, baking powder and salt in medium bowl. Using electric mixer, beat eggs, brown sugar, oil and vanilla in large bowl until smooth, about 3 minutes. Gradually stir in flour mixture; blend well. Spoon into prepared pan, spreading evenly. Bake until brown and cake springs back when touched in center, about 35 minutes. Cool completely in pan. Cut into bars. Store in airtight container.

Date-Nut Bars

For a crunchier bar, bake these the full 25 minutes.

Makes about 4 dozen

1 cup all purpose flour
¹/₂ teaspoon salt
¹/₄ teaspoon baking powder
1 cup sugar
1 cup chopped walnuts

1 cup chopped dates
2 eggs, beaten
¹/₄ cup (¹/₂ stick) butter, melted
1 teaspoon vanilla
Powdered sugar

Preheat oven to 350°F. Grease 9 × 13-inch jelly roll pan. Line with foil; grease foil and set aside.

Sift flour, salt and baking powder into medium bowl. Add all remaining ingredients except powdered sugar and mix well. Pour into pan, spreading evenly. Bake until golden, about 20 to 25 minutes. Invert onto work surface and carefully remove foil. Slice into bars while still warm. Sprinkle powdered sugar over top. Transfer bars to rack and let cool. Store in airtight container.

Triple Layer Bars

For best flavor, let these cookies mellow for two days before serving.

Makes about 12 dozen

Nut Filling
1¹/₂ pounds pecans
³/₄ cup sugar
1 teaspoon cinnamon

Pastry
5 cups sifted all purpose flour
1¹/₄ cups (2¹/₂ sticks) well-chilled unsalted butter, cut into 10 pieces
1 cup plus 2 tablespoons sugar
1 tablespoon baking soda

2¹/₂ teaspoons baking powder
5 egg yolks
¹/₃ cup sour cream
2 tablespoons bourbon
1 tablespoon vanilla

1 cup (10 ounces) seedless red raspberry preserves
1¹/₄ cups (12 ounces) apricot jam, pressed through sieve
1 egg white

For filling: Finely grind ¹/₂ pound pecans, ¹/₄ cup sugar and ¹/₃ teaspoon cinnamon in processor. Transfer to small bowl. Repeat with remaining ingredients in 2 more batches, transferring each to separate bowl.

For pastry: Place flour in work bowl of processor. (For standard size processor, prepare pastry in 2 batches.) Arrange butter in circle atop flour. Process

From Top: Fruit
Doughnuts with Berry
Sauce; Ice Cream
Trumpettes

Brian Leatart

From left to right: Copenhagen; Pasta Fleura; Chocolate Baklava

*From bottom: Hazelnut Balls; Blueberry
Bublanina; Great-Grandma Vratny's Jelly Puffs*

Left to right: Peanut Butter Favorites;
Glazed Apple Gems; Apricot Bars;
Date-Nut Goodies

Speculaas

Chocolate-dipped Sandwich Wafers

Mae Goodman's Hungarian
Coffee Crescents

20 seconds, stopping once to scrape down sides of work bowl. Add sugar, baking soda and baking powder. Blend until well mixed, using 12 to 15 on/off turns and stopping once to scrape down sides of bowl. Whisk yolks, sour cream, bourbon and vanilla in small bowl to blend. Pour in circle over dry ingredients. Blend using 5 or 6 on/off turns. Scrape down sides of work bowl. Process just until ball forms.

Preheat oven to 350°F. Grease 10 × 15-inch jelly roll pan. Divide pastry into 3 pieces. Roll 1 piece out between sheets of waxed paper to 10 × 15-inch rectangle. Place dough in prepared pan, discarding paper. Trim edges. Spread raspberry preserves over pastry. Lightly press 1 portion of nut filling into preserves. Roll out second piece of pastry and place in pan. Top with apricot jam and second portion of nut filling. Roll out last piece of dough and place over nuts. Beat egg white with fork until very foamy. Spread generously over dough. Sprinkle evenly with last portion of nut mixture. Pat nuts gently to secure.

Bake pastry until tester inserted in center comes out clean, about 45 minutes. Cool completely in pan. Cover and let stand overnight to mellow. Cut into 1-inch squares, wiping knife between each cut. Store in airtight container. (*Can be prepared ahead and stored at room temperature 5 days or frozen 2 months. Thaw on rack.*)

Cinnamon Bars

Makes about 3 dozen

1 cup (2 sticks) butter, room temperature
1 cup sugar
1 teaspoon vanilla

1 egg, separated
Pinch of salt
2 cups all purpose flour
2 teaspoons cinnamon

Preheat oven to 350°F. Grease 10 × 15-inch jelly roll pan. Cream butter with sugar in large bowl. Add vanilla. Mix in yolk and salt. Combine flour and cinnamon and stir into butter mixture. Pat evenly into prepared pan. Brush top with egg white to glaze. Bake until lightly browned, about 20 minutes. Cool slightly. Cut into bars. Store Cinnamon Bars in an airtight container.

Ginger Parkins

At serving time, spread the cut edges of these Scottish treats with butter. For maximum flavor, bake them one day ahead.

Makes about 4 dozen

1 cup all purpose flour
1 teaspoon ground ginger
3/4 teaspoon baking soda
1/2 teaspoon cinnamon
1/2 teaspoon allspice
1/2 teaspoon salt
1 cup firmly packed brown sugar

1/2 cup dark molasses
5 tablespoons unsalted butter
1/3 cup milk
1 egg, beaten to blend

Preheat oven to 350°F. Line 10 × 15-inch jelly roll pan with parchment. Mix first 6 ingredients in medium bowl. Stir sugar, molasses and butter in heavy small saucepan over low heat until butter melts. Mix into dry ingredients. Combine milk and egg and gently stir into batter. Spread mixture evenly in prepared pan. Bake 15 minutes. Reduce temperature to 325°F. Continue baking until center springs back when touched, 10 to 15 minutes. Cool in pan on rack. Cover with waxed paper. Let stand at room temperature overnight. Just before serving, cut into 3 × 1/2-inch strips.

Orkney Broonies

This traditional Scottish biscuit is similar to gingerbread. These are best when refrigerated at least one day.

Makes about 2 dozen

1 cup quick-cooking oats
¹/₂ cup all purpose flour
¹/₂ cup (1 stick) unsalted butter
¹/₂ cup firmly packed light brown sugar
2 teaspoons ground ginger
¹/₂ teaspoon baking powder
¹/₂ teaspoon baking soda
¹/₂ teaspoon salt
²/₃ cup buttermilk
¹/₄ cup light corn syrup
¹/₄ cup dark molasses
1 egg, room temperature

Preheat oven to 350°F. Lightly grease 8- or 9-inch square baking pan. Combine oats and flour in large bowl. Rub in butter until coarse meal forms. Mix in sugar, ginger, baking powder, baking soda and salt. Combine buttermilk, corn syrup, molasses and egg; gently blend into dry ingredients. Turn batter into prepared pan. Bake until center is firm to touch, 30 to 35 minutes. Cool in pan on rack. Cover and chill overnight. (*Can be prepared 1 week ahead.*) Cut into 1 × 2-inch bars.

Iced Spice Bars

Makes about 4 dozen bars

1¹/₂ cups all purpose flour
1 cup sugar
¹/₂ cup milk
¹/₂ cup vegetable oil
2 eggs
1 teaspoon salt
1 teaspoon baking soda
1 teaspoon cinnamon
1 teaspoon ground cloves
¹/₂ cup chopped pecans or walnuts
¹/₂ cup raisins

Icing
1 cup powdered sugar
¹/₂ cup hot water

Preheat oven to 375°F. Grease 10 × 15-inch jelly roll pan. Combine first 9 ingredients in large bowl and mix well. Stir in nuts and raisins. Turn batter into prepared pan, spreading evenly. Bake until golden, about 20 minutes. Cool bars in pan on rack 10 minutes.

For icing: Blend powdered sugar and water in small bowl until smooth. Cover bars evenly with icing. Cool completely before slicing. Store in airtight container.

Congo Bars

Congo Bars freeze well.

Makes 32 bars

¹/₂ cup plus 2 tablespoons (1¹/₄ sticks) unsalted butter, room temperature
2¹/₃ cups firmly packed dark brown sugar
3 eggs
2¹/₂ cups unbleached all purpose flour
2 teaspoons baking powder
¹/₄ teaspoon salt
1 12-ounce package semisweet chocolate chips
¹/₂ cup chopped walnuts

Preheat oven to 350°F. Grease 10 × 15-inch jelly roll pan. Beat butter with sugar in large bowl until light and creamy. Add eggs one at a time, beating well after each addition. Stir in flour, baking powder and salt and blend well. Fold in chips and chopped nuts.

Turn into prepared pan, spreading evenly. Bake until top is lightly browned, about 20 to 25 minutes. Transfer to wire rack and let cool. Cut into bars. Store in airtight container.

Chocolate and Butterscotch Bars

Makes about 36

1/2 cup (1 stick) unsalted butter
1 1/2 cups graham cracker crumbs
1 cup semisweet chocolate chips
1 cup butterscotch chips

1 1/3 cups shredded coconut
1 cup toasted hazelnuts, chopped
1 14-ounce can sweetened
 condensed milk

Preheat oven to 350°F. Place butter in 9 × 13-inch baking pan and melt in oven. Swirl pan to coat bottom and sides with butter. Spread crumbs evenly over bottom of pan. Layer chocolate chips, butterscotch chips, coconut and nuts over crumbs. Pour condensed milk over nuts. Bake until edges are golden brown, about 25 minutes. Cool completely. Cut into bars.

Chocolate Chip Mincemeat Bars

Makes 36

2 cups all purpose flour
2 teaspoons baking soda

1 cup (2 sticks) butter, room
 temperature
1 cup sugar
3 eggs

1 1/2 cups mincemeat
2 cups chopped pitted dates
1 12-ounce package semisweet
 chocolate chips
1 cup chopped walnuts

Preheat oven to 350°F. Butter 11 × 17 × 3/4-inch jelly roll pan. Combine flour and baking soda in bowl; set aside.

Cream butter with sugar using electric mixer. Add eggs 1 at a time. Add mincemeat in batches, alternating with flour mixture. Fold in dates, chocolate chips and nuts. Spread evenly in prepared pan. Bake until tester inserted in center comes out clean, about 30 minutes. Cool to room temperature. Cut into bars to serve.

Chocolate Apricot Bars

This nutty, rum-laced confection does not require any baking.

Makes about 4 dozen

Apricot Filling
2/3 cup dried apricots
1/4 cup water
5 tablespoons powdered sugar
2 1/2 tablespoons well-chilled unsalted
 butter, chopped
1 1/2 teaspoons dark rum

Nut Layer
6 ounces blanched whole almonds
1/3 cup powdered sugar

4 ounces bittersweet or semisweet
 chocolate, coarsely chopped
2 tablespoons dark rum
1 egg white

1 cup chocolate sprinkles

For filling: Combine apricots and water in heavy small saucepan and bring to boil. Reduce heat to low and cook uncovered until water is absorbed, stirring frequently, about 5 minutes. Puree apricots and 2 tablespoons powdered sugar in processor until smooth, stopping once to scrape down sides of work bowl. Set aside 1 tablespoon puree for pastry. Add remaining 3 tablespoons sugar, butter and rum to processor. Blend until smooth, stopping once to scrape down sides of work bowl, 5 to 10 seconds. Transfer to small bowl and set aside.

For nut layer: Finely chop almonds in processor. Add powdered sugar and bittersweet chocolate. Process until finely ground. Add rum, egg white and 1 tablespoon reserved apricot puree. Process until sticky dough forms.

Divide dough in half. Roll one piece out between sheets of waxed paper to 7 × 11-inch rectangle. Gently push sides toward center with spatula to square off. Remove top sheet of paper. Cover dough with half of chocolate sprinkles. Press with rolling pin. Invert dough onto baking sheet. Discard paper. Freeze dough until firm, about 5 minutes. Spread filling evenly over dough. Freeze until firm, 15 minutes.

Roll out remaining dough between sheets of waxed paper to 7 × 11-inch rectangle. Invert atop filling, removing paper. Cover with remaining sprinkles. Press in lightly with rolling pin. Square sides of pastry with spatula. Freeze until firm, 10 to 15 minutes.

Cut pastry into 1³/₄ × ³/₄-inch bars. Store in airtight container. (*Can be prepared 1 week ahead and refrigerated or frozen for up to 3 weeks.*)

Oatmeal Fudge Bars

Makes about 5 dozen

1 cup (2 sticks) margarine, room temperature
2 cups firmly packed light brown sugar
2 eggs
3 cups rolled oats
2¹/₂ cups all purpose flour
2 teaspoons vanilla
1 teaspoon baking soda
1 teaspoon salt
1 cup chopped walnuts

1 14-ounce can sweetened condensed milk
1 12-ounce package semisweet chocolate chips
1¹/₂ cups chopped walnuts
2 tablespoons (¹/₄ stick) margarine
2 teaspoons vanilla
¹/₂ teaspoon salt

Generously grease 10 × 15 × 2-inch baking pan. Cream 1 cup margarine with sugar in large bowl. Add eggs one at a time, beating well after each addition. Mix in oats, flour, vanilla, baking soda and salt. Stir in 1 cup walnuts. Set aside.

Combine milk and chocolate in top of double boiler set over hot water and stir until chocolate melts. Add remaining ingredients and blend well.

Preheat oven to 350°F. Spoon ²/₃ of oat mixture into prepared pan, compacting with fork. Spread chocolate mixture over top. Crumble remaining oat mixture over chocolate and spread with fork. Bake until golden, 25 to 30 minutes. Cool. Cut into 1¹/₂-inch bars.

Chewy Butterscotch Bars

Makes about 2 dozen

²/₃ cup firmly packed brown sugar
¹/₂ cup (1 stick) butter, room temperature
2 eggs, room temperature
1 teaspoon vanilla
³/₄ cup rolled oats
¹/₂ cup all purpose flour

1 3³/₄-ounce package instant butterscotch pudding mix
¹/₄ teaspoon salt
³/₄ cup golden raisins
Powdered sugar

Preheat oven to 350°F. Grease 9 × 9-inch baking pan. Combine brown sugar, butter, eggs and vanilla in large bowl and beat well. Add oats, flour, pudding mix and salt and mix thoroughly. Stir in raisins. Spread batter in prepared pan. Bake until lightly golden, about 35 minutes. Cool in pan on wire rack. Sprinkle with powdered sugar. Cut into bars. Store bars in airtight container.

Chocolate Nut Brownies

Bake these in minutes in the microwave.

Makes about 20 brownies

2 ounces unsweetened baking chocolate
1/2 cup (1 stick) unsalted butter

2 eggs
3/4 cup sugar
1/2 cup all purpose flour
1 tablespoon vanilla

1 teaspoon baking powder
1/4 teaspoon salt
1 cup coarsely chopped walnuts
1 cup chocolate chips
Powdered sugar (optional)

Combine chocolate and butter in 2-quart measuring cup and cook on High until butter is melted, about 1 1/2 minutes. Stir to blend (chocolate will not appear melted until you stir).

Beat eggs in large bowl until well mixed. Add chocolate mixture, sugar, flour, vanilla, baking powder and salt and blend thoroughly. Stir in nuts and chocolate chips. Turn into 9-inch pie plate or quiche dish. Cook on High for 6 minutes (mixture will still be moist, but will firm as it cools). Sprinkle with powdered sugar. Let cool completely before cutting into squares.

Glazed Chocolate Pecan Brownies

Makes 2 dozen

3 ounces unsweetened chocolate
1/2 cup (1 stick) unsalted butter, room temperature
1 cup sugar
1/2 cup firmly packed light brown sugar
1/2 cup light corn syrup

4 eggs, room temperature
1 cup bread flour
1 cup pecan halves

6 tablespoons whipping cream
4 ounces semisweet chocolate, chopped

Preheat oven to 375°F. Butter and flour 13 × 9 × 2-inch baking pan. Melt 3 ounces chocolate in top of double boiler set over gently simmering water. Cream butter with sugars in large bowl of electric mixer. Blend in corn syrup. Beat in eggs 1 at a time. Stir in melted chocolate. Gently fold in flour and pecans; do not overmix. Pour into prepared pan. Bake until set, 25 to 30 minutes. Cool completely in pan on rack.

Bring cream to boil in heavy small saucepan. Remove from heat. Add 4 ounces chocolate and stir until melted. Cool to room temperature. Spread glaze evenly over brownies in pan. Refrigerate until firm. Cut into squares and serve.

Hazelnut Chocolate Chunk Brownies

Serve with a white chocolate ice cream for a superb combination.

Makes about 4 dozen

Butter
- 1 cup (2 sticks) unsalted butter
- 2 cups sugar
- 4 eggs, beaten to blend
- 1/2 cup unsweetened cocoa powder (preferably imported)
- 1 tablespoon vanilla
- 1/3 cup all purpose flour

- 1/2 teaspoon salt
- 7 ounces imported bittersweet or semisweet chocolate, coarsely chopped
- 1/2 cup hazelnuts, toasted, husked and coarsely chopped

Preheat oven to 350°F. Lightly butter 9 × 13-inch baking pan. Melt 1 cup butter in heavy large saucepan over low heat. Remove from heat and whisk in sugar, eggs, cocoa and vanilla. Stir in flour and salt. Add chopped chocolate and nuts. Spread batter in prepared pan. Bake until tester inserted in center comes out barely moist but not wet, 25 to 30 minutes. Cool in pan on rack. (*Can be prepared 1 day ahead. Wrap tightly.*) Cut into 1 1/2-inch squares.

Chocolate Fudgy Brownies

Makes 16 brownies

- 1/2 cup (1 stick) butter
- 2 ounces (2 squares) unsweetened chocolate
- 1 cup sugar
- 1/2 cup all purpose flour

- 1/2 teaspoon baking powder
- 2 eggs
- 1 teaspoon vanilla
- 1/2 cup chopped walnuts

Preheat oven to 450°F. Grease 8-inch square baking pan. Melt butter with chocolate in medium saucepan. Remove from heat. Combine sugar, flour and baking powder in large bowl. Add eggs and vanilla and beat well. Pour in chocolate mixture and blend thoroughly. Stir in walnuts. Pour into pan. Bake until tester inserted in center comes out clean, about 15 to 20 minutes. Cool completely in pan before slicing.

Toffee Fudge Brownies

These are dark, moist and crunchy with bits of toffee candy.

Makes twenty-five 1 3/4-inch squares

- 6 chocolate-covered toffee bars (6 3/8 ounces total), broken into small pieces
- 1 cup walnut pieces
- 1 1/4 cups sugar
- 5 ounces unsweetened chocolate, broken into pieces

- 1/2 cup (1 stick) unsalted butter, cut into 4 pieces, room temperature
- 4 eggs
- 1 tablespoon vanilla
- 1/4 teaspoon salt
- 2/3 cup unbleached all purpose flour

Position rack in center of oven and preheat to 325°F. Grease and flour 9-inch square baking pan.

Combine toffee and walnuts in processor and chop coarsely using 6 to 8 on/off turns. Remove from work bowl and set aside. Combine sugar and chocolate in work bowl and mix using 6 on/off turns, then process until chocolate is as fine as sugar, about 1 minute. Add butter and blend 1 minute. Add eggs, vanilla and salt and blend until fluffy, about 40 seconds, stopping as necessary to scrape down sides of work bowl. Add flour and toffee mixture and blend using 4 to 5 on/off turns, just until flour is incorporated; do not overprocess (remove steel knife and blend mixture gently with spatula if necessary to mix in flour completely). Turn batter into prepared pan, spreading evenly. Bake until tester inserted in center comes out almost clean, about 50 minutes (for firmer, cakelike brownies, bake about 5 minutes longer). Let cool in pan on rack. Cut into 1³/4-inch squares. Store in airtight container.

Bronxville Brownies

Makes about 2 dozen

¹/4 cup (¹/2 stick) margarine, room temperature
1 cup sugar
1 egg, beaten to blend
¹/2 cup all purpose flour

¹/2 cup chopped pecans *or* walnuts
2 ounces unsweetened chocolate, melted
¹/4 teaspoon salt

Preheat oven to 350°F. Grease 9 × 9-inch ovenproof glass dish. Cream margarine with sugar in large bowl. Stir in egg. Mix in remaining ingredients. Spoon into prepared pan, spreading evenly. Bake until tester inserted in center comes out clean, 20 to 25 minutes; do not overbake (brownies should be moist). Cool in pan. Cut into squares and serve.

Brownies with Peanut Butter and Caramel Filling

A great combination of flavors. These are best served the same day as baked.

Makes 3 dozen

Filling
1 cup extra-chunky peanut butter
¹/2 cup plus 2 tablespoons caramel ice cream topping
1 egg yolk

Brownie Batter
Butter
¹/2 cup (1 stick) unsalted butter, room temperature
3 ounces unsweetened chocolate

³/4 cup sifted all purpose flour
¹/4 cup unsweetened cocoa powder
¹/2 teaspoon baking powder
¹/4 teaspoon salt
1 cup firmly packed dark brown sugar
¹/2 cup sugar
3 extra-large eggs, room temperature

For filling: Combine all ingredients in medium bowl. Cover and refrigerate while preparing brownie batter.

For batter: Butter bottom of 9-inch square baking pan. Melt ¹/2 cup butter and chocolate in top of double boiler over barely simmering water. Stir until smooth. Cool 15 minutes.

Sift together flour, cocoa powder, baking powder and salt. Using electric mixer, beat both sugars and eggs until thick and fluffy. Gently fold in melted chocolate mixture, then dry ingredients. Pour half of batter into prepared pan, smoothing surface. Freeze batter for 15 minutes to firm.

Position rack in center of oven and preheat to 325°F. Form filling into thirty-six ³/4-inch balls. Flatten each into 1-inch circle. Arrange atop brownie layer in 6 rows of 6, pressing lightly so circles adhere. Spoon remaining brownie batter evenly over filling. Cover tightly with foil. Bake 30 minutes. Remove foil and continue baking until tester inserted between mounds of filling comes out with only a few crumbs clinging to it, about 35 minutes. Cool completely in pan on rack. Cut into 1¹/2-inch squares. Store brownies in airtight container.

Another Better Brownie

Serve these topped with big scoops of vanilla ice cream.

8 servings

1 cup sugar
²/₃ cup unbleached all purpose flour
¹/₂ cup unsweetened cocoa powder
¹/₂ teaspoon baking powder
¹/₂ cup (1 stick) butter, cut into 8 pieces

2 eggs, beaten to blend
1 teaspoon vanilla
¹/₂ cup frozen milk chocolate chips
¹/₂ cup chopped walnuts

Preheat oven to 350°F. Generously grease 8-inch square baking pan. Combine sugar, flour, cocoa and baking powder in food processor and sift using 2 to 3 on/off turns. With machine running, drop butter through feed tube 1 piece at a time and process until mixture resembles coarse meal. Add eggs and vanilla. Blend just until dough starts to come together. Add chocolate chips and nuts and process until just mixed, using 4 to 5 on/off turns. Spread batter evenly in prepared pan. Bake until tester inserted in center comes out clean, about 30 minutes. Cool slightly.

Mississippi Mud

Children will be enchanted with this fanciful chocolate dessert.

12 servings

Brownie
1 cup (2 sticks) unsalted butter, room temperature
2 cups sugar
4 eggs, room temperature
1 teaspoon vanilla
1¹/₂ cups unbleached all purpose flour
3 tablespoons unsweetened cocoa powder
1¹/₂ cups flaked coconut
1¹/₂ cups pecans or walnuts, finely chopped

1 7-ounce jar marshmallow cream

Frosting
¹/₂ cup (1 stick) unsalted butter, room temperature
1 teaspoon vanilla
4 cups powdered sugar
¹/₃ cup unsweetened cocoa powder
¹/₂ cup evaporated milk

For brownie: Preheat oven to 350°F. Grease 9 × 13-inch baking pan. Cream butter with sugar in large bowl of electric mixer until light and fluffy. Beat in eggs 1 at a time. Blend in vanilla. Combine flour and cocoa powder. Beat dry ingredients into butter mixture. Fold in coconut and pecans. Spoon batter into prepared pan, spreading evenly. Bake until tester inserted in center comes out clean, 30 to 40 minutes.

Immediately spoon marshmallow cream over brownie. As cream begins to melt, spread gently. Cool brownie completely.

For frosting: Cream butter and vanilla in large bowl of electric mixer. Combine sugar and cocoa powder. Gradually beat into butter mixture, alternating with milk. Continue beating until frosting is light and fluffy, 3 to 5 minutes. Spread frosting over brownie. Cut into squares to serve.

Scotch Shortbread

8 servings

1¼ cups all purpose flour
¼ cup sugar
½ cup (1 stick) butter, cubed, room temperature

3 tablespoons cornstarch
1 tablespoon sugar

Preheat oven to 375°F. Combine first 4 ingredients in medium bowl and blend until finely crumbled. Pat dough into 8- to 9-inch baking pan with removable bottom, spreading evenly. Press edges with tines of fork; gently prick bottom. Bake until lightly golden, about 25 minutes. Cool in pan 5 minutes. Cut into wedges using sharp knife. Sprinkle top with remaining sugar. Let cool completely in pan before serving, about 30 minutes.

Liesbeth's Butter Cake

Similar to a sweet shortbread, this rich pastry is an old Dutch favorite.

6 to 8 servings

2 cups flour
1½ cups sugar
1 cup (2 sticks) unsalted butter, melted

1 egg, separated

Preheat oven to 450°F. Sift flour and sugar together in medium bowl. Pour in butter and blend well. Add yolk and knead thoroughly. Press into 9-inch metal pie pan. Brush lightly with beaten egg white. Bake 15 minutes. Reduce oven temperature to 225°F and continue baking until top is golden and edges are browned, about 15 to 20 minutes. Cool before cutting. Use sharp thin knife to slice into thin wedges.

Almond Shortbread

Makes about 16

1¼ cups all purpose flour
¼ cup sugar
¼ cup finely ground toasted almonds

½ cup (1 stick) butter, cut into small pieces
Slivered almonds
1 tablespoon sugar

Preheat oven to 325°F. Combine first 3 ingredients in large bowl. Cut in butter until mixture forms coarse meal. Gather dough into ball. Press evenly into 8 × 8-inch pan. Pierce all over with fork. Score surface, forming 1½-inch squares (do not cut through). Gently press in slivered almonds. Bake until shortbread is golden brown, about 40 minutes. Immediately cut along score lines. Sprinkle top with 1 tablespoon sugar. Cool in pan on rack.

Raisin Shortbread

*A nice twist on
Scottish shortbread.*

Makes 8

¹/₃ cup fresh orange juice
³/₄ cup raisins
³/₄ cup (1¹/₂ sticks) unsalted butter,
room temperature

¹/₄ cup sugar
1¹/₂ cups all purpose flour
¹/₄ teaspoon salt

Preheat oven to 300°F. Lightly grease baking sheet and dust with flour. Bring orange juice to boil in heavy small saucepan. Add raisins. Reduce heat and simmer until liquid is reduced to 1 tablespoon, about 5 minutes. Cool completely.

Mix butter and sugar in medium bowl until smooth. Blend in flour and salt. Gently mix in raisins and orange juice. Shape dough into smooth ball. Transfer to prepared sheet and press into 8-inch circle. Score surface to form 8 wedges, using small knife. Pierce each wedge twice with fork. Bake shortbread until golden brown, 40 to 45 minutes. Cut wedges apart while hot. Cool completely in pan on rack. Store shortbread in airtight container.

Orange Shortbread Wedges with Mincemeat Filling

Makes 22

2¹/₄ cups all purpose flour
³/₄ teaspoon salt
³/₄ cup superfine sugar
4 teaspoons finely grated
orange peel
1 cup (2 sticks) unsalted butter,
room temperature
1 tablespoon orange liqueur
2 teaspoons fresh orange juice

1 teaspoon fresh lemon juice
1 teaspoon vanilla
3 drops of orange extract

3 gingersnap cookies, crushed to
crumbs
6 ounces condensed mincemeat,
finely crumbled

Line baking sheet with foil. Draw 10-inch circle on foil. Line another baking sheet with parchment. Draw 10-inch circle on paper. Combine flour and salt. Mix sugar and peel in processor 10 seconds. Using electric mixer, cream butter with sugar mixture in large bowl. Using spatula, blend in liqueur, juices, vanilla and orange extract. Fold in flour mixture.

Divide dough in half. Wrap and refrigerate 1 half. Press remainder onto foil circle. Refrigerate. Press other half onto parchment circle. Sprinkle with gingersnap crumbs. Sprinkle with mincemeat. Invert dough on foil circle atop mincemeat. Peel off foil. Press dough firmly. Seal edges to enclose filling; straighten shortbread edges.

Position rack in center of oven and preheat to 300°F. Draw 5-inch circle (about 2¹/₂ inches in from edge) in center of shortbread. Using small sharp knife, cut straight up and down through shortbread to mark off circle. Cut inner circle into 6 wedges. Cut thin outer circle into 16 wedges. Using toothpick, pierce 4 holes in each wedge. Attach inverted 10-inch springform ring around shortbread. Press dough up against sides to form perfect circle. Using tines of fork, press decoratively around edges of outer and inner circles. Bake 30 minutes. Remove springform. Continue baking until outside edges are lightly golden, 10 to 15 minutes. Slide parchment onto rack. Using small sharp knife, cut straight up and down to mark off wedges; do not separate. Cool completely. Wrap in foil. Let stand 1 day. Separate into wedges before serving.

Apricot-Filled Italian Shortbread

A delicious dessert or breakfast treat.

Makes 25 two-inch squares

Apricot Filling
- 1 cup dried apricots, coarsely chopped
- 1 cup dry white wine
- 2/3 cup sugar

Pastry
- 1 1/2 cups all purpose flour
- 1/4 cup cake flour
- 14 tablespoons (1 3/4 sticks) unsalted butter, room temperature
- 1 cup sugar

- 1 egg, room temperature
- 1 teaspoon almond extract
- 1 teaspoon vanilla

Topping
- 1 egg white, room temperature
- 1 1/2 cups sliced almonds, toasted
- 1/3 cup plus 1 tablespoon sugar

For filling: Combine apricots, wine and sugar in small nonaluminum saucepan. Let mixture stand 1 hour.

Bring apricot mixture to boil. Reduce heat to medium-low, cover and cook 10 minutes. Uncover, increase heat to medium and cook, stirring frequently, until thick and dense, about 10 minutes. Cool completely. Cover and refrigerate until ready to use. (*Can be prepared up to 4 days ahead.*)

For pastry: Sift flours together. Using electric mixer, cream butter until fluffy. Gradually beat in sugar and continue mixing until fluffy, 2 to 3 minutes. Blend in egg, almond extract and vanilla. Using large spoon, gently fold in flour mixture. Turn dough out onto surface. Divide in half. Flatten each into square. Wrap in plastic. Refrigerate at least 2 hours.

For topping: Set aside 1 teaspoon egg white. Transfer remainder to processor or blender. Add sliced almonds and sugar and mix to paste.

To assemble: Position rack in center of oven and preheat to 325°F. Butter and flour 10-inch square baking pan. Roll 1 piece of dough out on lightly floured surface into 10-inch square. Line prepared pan with dough, gently pushing into corners. Moisten edges with reserved 1 teaspoon white. Spread filling over dough, leaving 1/4-inch border. Roll remaining dough out on lightly floured surface into 10-inch square. Set atop filling. Using side of hand, gently press sides down to seal. Dot entire surface of pastry with topping, using moistened spoon as aid. Bake until knife inserted in center comes out clean, 80 to 90 minutes. Cool in pan on rack. Cut into 2-inch squares. (*Can be prepared 2 days ahead. Store in airtight container in cool dry place.*)

Millionaire's Shortbread

A Scottish teatime favorite, this shortbread is topped with caramel and chocolate.

Makes about 5 dozen

Shortbread
- 1/2 cup pastry flour
- 1/2 cup all purpose flour
- 1/3 cup superfine sugar
- 7 tablespoons well-chilled unsalted butter, cut into small pieces

Caramel
- 1/4 cup (1/2 stick) unsalted butter
- 1/2 cup firmly packed dark brown sugar

- 3 tablespoons light corn syrup
- 1/4 cup whipping cream

- 6 ounces semisweet chocolate, melted

Preheat oven to 375°F. Combine flours and sugar in processor. Blend in butter using on/off turns until mixture is crumbly. Pat into bottom of 8 × 8 × 2-inch baking pan. Bake until shortbread just begins to color, 13 to 14 minutes. Remove from oven.

For caramel: Melt butter in heavy medium saucepan over low heat. Add sugar and corn syrup. Cook, swirling pan occasionally, until sugar melts. Increase heat to medium and cook until mixture registers 255°F on candy thermometer (hard-ball stage), stirring constantly. Cool 30 seconds; stir in cream (be careful; mixture may bubble). Return pan to medium heat and stir until mixture registers 235°F on candy thermometer (soft-ball stage). Pour hot caramel over shortbread. Cool to room temperature.

Spread melted chocolate evenly over caramel. Freeze until chocolate is firm, 10 to 15 minutes. Cut into 1-inch squares. Store in airtight container in cool place or refrigerator.

Spiced Yogurt Diamonds

Makes about 12

1½ cups sugar
½ cup (1 stick) unsalted butter, room temperature
2 eggs, room temperature
2½ cups all purpose flour
1 teaspoon baking soda
   Pinch of salt
1 cup plain yogurt
1 teaspoon vanilla

½ cup dried currants
½ teaspoon freshly grated nutmeg
½ teaspoon cinnamon
¼ teaspoon ground cloves

Preheat oven to 350°F. Butter 9-inch square baking pan. Using electric mixer, beat sugar and butter until fluffy. Beat in eggs 1 at a time. Sift flour, baking soda and salt together. Combine yogurt and vanilla in small cup. Stir dry ingredients and yogurt alternately into butter mixture. Pour half of batter into prepared pan. Combine currants and spices. Sprinkle over batter in pan. Top with remaining batter. Bake cake until springy to touch, about 40 minutes. Cool completely on rack. Cut into 2-inch diamonds.

Blarney Stones

Little pieces of cake coated with frosting and rolled in nuts, these are a St. Patrick's Day favorite you can enjoy throughout the year.

Makes 24

4 eggs, separated
1¼ cups sugar
2 cups all purpose flour
1 cup boiling water
2 teaspoons baking powder
1 teaspoon vanilla

2¼ cups powdered sugar
1¼ cups (2½ sticks) butter, room temperature
1 teaspoon milk
1 1-pound jar salted peanuts, finely chopped

Preheat oven to 350°F. Cream yolks and 1¼ cups sugar in large bowl. Mix in flour, ½ cup boiling water and baking powder. Add remaining water and vanilla and blend well. Beat whites until stiff but not dry. Fold whites into batter. Pour batter into ungreased 9 × 13-inch baking pan. Bake until tester inserted in center comes out clean, 30 minutes. Cool in pan on rack.

Cream powdered sugar and butter. Blend in milk. Cut cake into 24 squares. Spread icing over top, bottom and sides of squares. Roll in finely chopped peanuts to cover completely. Store in refrigerator.

6 ❧ *Small Pastries*

The irresistible treats featured here combine the best of two favorites: the flavors and textures of big showstopping desserts with the lovely individual size of a cookie. Of particular note here are the intriguing international specialties, including Swedish Toscaboard (page 103), Moravian Sugar Cakes (page 108) and jam-filled Pasta Fleura (page 103). Kadaife with Citrus and Nuts (page 112) is made from a textured Greek pastry dough that resembles shredded wheat. Sheets of Greek phyllo are used in several recipes, such as Chocolate Baklava (page 110), a delectable variation on the classic dessert, and the light and flaky pastry cups for Cranberry-Hazelnut Phyllo Baskets (page 109).

Fruit pastries are always popular, and festive Berry Pizzas (page 105) are sure to be the hit of any party. Doughnuts are also terrific, especially when presented with a fruit sauce: Fresh Fruit Doughnuts with Berry Sauce (page 113) are a good example. Great-Grandma Vratny's Jelly Puffs (page 112) are delectable jelly-filled cakes ideal for brunch. But, actually, the tempting pastries in this chapter will dress up any occasion, no matter what time of day.

Flaky Date Pastries

A delightful treat with hot tea. These taste best the day they are baked, but can be assembled ahead and frozen.

Makes about 25

Date Paste

- 1/2 pound pitted chopped dates
- 1 cup water
- 1/2 cup (1 stick) unsalted butter, cut into 8 pieces
- 2 tablespoons fresh lemon juice
- 1 teaspoon cinnamon
- 1 teaspoon vanilla

Pastry

- 2 cups all purpose flour
- 1 teaspoon salt
- 2/3 cup well-chilled unsalted butter, cut into tablespoons
- 1 egg, beaten to blend
- 3 to 4 tablespoons cold water

- 1 egg beaten with 2 tablespoons water (glaze)

For dates: Simmer dates with water in heavy medium saucepan until water evaporates, stirring occasionally, about 12 minutes. Continue stirring over medium-low heat until thick, sticky paste forms, about 5 minutes. Add butter and stir until mixture pulls away from sides of pan, about 6 minutes. Remove from heat and mix in lemon juice, cinnamon and vanilla. Spread paste out on platter and cool. Refrigerate until very firm.

For pastry: Blend flour and salt in processor. Cut in butter until coarse meal forms, using on/off turns. Combine 1 egg with 3 tablespoons water. With machine running, pour egg mixture in through feed tube. Continue mixing just until dough forms small beads, using on/off turns and adding remaining 1 tablespoon water if necessary. Gather dough into ball; flatten into disc. Wrap and refrigerate 30 minutes.

Preheat oven to 400°F. Roll dough out on lightly floured surface to thickness of 1/8 inch. Cut out 2-inch rounds, using cookie cutter or glass. Gather scraps and refrigerate briefly to firm. Reroll dough and cut out additional rounds. Place 1 teaspoon date paste in center of half of dough rounds. Top each with another round; press edges to flatten and seal. Crimp edges. Arrange pastries on ungreased baking sheet. (*Can be prepared 1 week ahead. Cover tightly and freeze. Do not thaw before baking.*) Brush pastries lightly with glaze. Bake until golden brown, about 20 minutes. Cool on rack. Serve pastries warm or at room temperature.

Fruit-Filled Dessert Squares

Makes about 1 1/2 dozen

- 1 cup (2 sticks) butter, room temperature
- 1 1/2 cups sugar
- 4 eggs
- 2 1/4 cups all purpose flour
- 1 tablespoon vanilla
- 1 21-ounce can fruit pie filling

  Powdered sugar (garnish)

Preheat oven to 350°F. Butter bottom and sides of 10 × 15-inch jelly roll pan. Cream butter with sugar in large bowl. Beat in eggs one at a time. Gradually stir in flour and vanilla. Turn batter into prepared pan, spreading evenly. Drop 30 large spoonfuls of pie filling over batter at equal intervals. Bake until golden, about 40 to 45 minutes. Cool slightly. Sprinkle with powdered sugar. Cut into squares before serving.

Pasta Fleura

This simple pastry is perfect with coffee or tea. For variation, spread half the pastry with cherry preserves and half with apricot preserves.

Makes about 50

¼ cup lukewarm water (95°F)
1 yeast cake
1½ cups (3 sticks) well-chilled unsalted butter
4 cups bleached all purpose flour
4 egg yolks
¼ cup milk

2 pounds cherry preserves
1 egg, beaten to blend (glaze)

Preheat oven to 350°F. Grease 11 × 16-inch baking pan. Combine water and yeast in small bowl; stir to dissolve. Cut butter into flour in processor until coarse meal forms. (If using standard-size processor, mix dough in 2 batches.) Add yeast, yolks and milk and process until ball forms.

Roll ⅔ of dough out on lightly floured surface to ³⁄₁₆-inch-thick rectangle. Transfer to prepared pan; trim edges. Spread with preserves. Roll remaining dough out on lightly floured surface to ³⁄₁₆-inch-thick rectangle. Cut into ¾-inch-wide strips. Arrange in lattice pattern atop preserves. Crimp edges to seal. Carefully brush lattice with glaze. Bake until pastry is golden brown, about 40 minutes. Cool. (*Can be prepared ahead. Wrap tightly and refrigerate 5 days or freeze 1 month. Bring to room temperature before serving.*) Cut into 2-inch squares to serve.

Toscaboard

Offer these crisp, nut-filled delights the same day they are baked.

8 to 10 servings

Crust
1¼ cups unbleached all purpose flour
¼ teaspoon salt
10 tablespoons (1¼ sticks) well-chilled unsalted butter, thinly sliced
3 tablespoons cold water

Topping
5 tablespoons unsalted butter
½ cup sugar
3 tablespoons half and half
4½ teaspoons all purpose flour
1 cup slivered almonds, toasted

For crust: Combine flour and salt in medium bowl. Cut in butter until coarse meal forms. Add water and mix just until dough holds together. Divide dough in half. Flatten each piece to 3 × 6-inch rectangle. Wrap in plastic and refrigerate at least 1 hour. (*Can be prepared 1 day ahead.*)

Position rack in center of oven and preheat to 400°F. Roll 1 piece of dough out on lightly floured cloth to 6 × 12-inch rectangle. Transfer to ungreased large baking sheet. Repeat with second piece of dough and transfer to same sheet. Pierce dough all over with fork. Fold outer ¾ inch of pastry in toward center forming double edge. Let stand at room temperature 15 minutes. Bake pastries until they are just beginning to color, piercing occasionally with fork if they puff, 10 to 12 minutes.

Meanwhile, for topping: Melt butter in heavy small saucepan over low heat. Add sugar, half and half and flour and whisk until sugar dissolves. Increase heat to medium-high and bring to boil, stirring constantly. Turn off heat and mix in almonds.

Immediately divide topping between crusts, spreading evenly. Return pastries to oven and bake until topping bubbles and is light golden brown, 15 to 17 minutes. Immediately cut pastries crosswise into 2-inch-wide strips. Serve warm or at room temperature.

Copenhagen

The sweet crust is filled with spiced ground almonds, then topped with crisp phyllo pastry. The cake was created in 1863 by a royal baker to honor the Danish monarch George I on his coronation as king of Greece.

Makes 24

Sweet Pastry
    1 cup (2 sticks) unsalted butter, room temperature
   11 tablespoons sugar
    1 egg
    1 teaspoon grated orange peel
  1/2 teaspoon vanilla
    3 cups cake flour

Almond Filling
    6 eggs, separated, room temperature
  1/2 cup sugar

    1 pound almonds, toasted and ground to coarse meal
    1 tablespoon orange liqueur
    1 teaspoon baking powder
    1 teaspoon cinnamon
    1 teaspoon almond extract
      Pinch of cream of tartar

   12 sheets phyllo pastry dough
  1/2 cup (1 stick) unsalted butter, melted
      Cinnamon Syrup*

For pastry: Using electric mixer, beat butter until light. Add sugar and beat until light and fluffy. Beat in egg, orange peel and vanilla. Slowly add flour and mix until soft dough forms. Gather dough into rectangle. Wrap in plastic and refrigerate 15 minutes.

Roll pastry out to 14 × 17-inch rectangle. Fit into 9 × 12-inch baking pan, bringing edges 1/4 inch above pan. Pierce with fork. Freeze 20 minutes.

Preheat oven to 400°F. Bake pastry until golden brown, 12 to 15 minutes. Cool. Reduce temperature to 350°F.

For filling: Using electric mixer, beat yolks until light. Gradually add sugar and beat until pale yellow and slowly dissolving ribbon forms when beaters are lifted. Fold in almonds, liqueur, baking powder, cinnamon and almond extract. Using clean, dry beaters, beat whites and cream of tartar in another bowl until stiff but not dry. Fold 1/4 of whites into yolks to lighten; fold in remaining whites. Spread in crust.

Stack pastry sheets and cut to fit top of pan. Place 1 sheet atop filling and brush with butter. Repeat with remaining pastry sheets. Tuck in edges. Score top 2 layers of phyllo with sharp knife, dividing into 24 diamond-shaped pieces. Bake until top is golden brown, about 1 hour. Pour cooled syrup over hot dessert. Cool completely. (*Can be prepared 3 days ahead. Wrap tightly and refrigerate. Bring to room temperature before serving.*) Cut pastry along score marks.

*Cinnamon Syrup

Makes about 2 cups

  2 1/4 cups sugar
  1 1/2 cups water

    2 3-inch cinnamon sticks
  1 1/2 teaspoons fresh lemon juice

Cook all ingredients in heavy medium saucepan over low heat, swirling pan occasionally, until sugar dissolves. Increase heat and boil gently 30 minutes. Cool completely. Discard cinnamon.

Berry Pizzas

Present these delicate pastries soon after baking. Leave them whole or cut into quarters.

Makes 6

Pastry
- ⅓ cup blanched almonds, lightly toasted
- 2 cups all purpose flour
- 14 tablespoons (1¾ sticks) butter, room temperature
- ¼ cup sugar
- 1 egg
- 1 teaspoon grated lemon peel
- 1 teaspoon baking powder

- 1⅓ cups fresh blueberries*
- 3 tablespoons sugar
- 1 teaspoon cornstarch
- 1⅓ cups fresh raspberries*
- 3 tablespoons sugar
- 1 teaspoon cornstarch
- Softly whipped cream

For dough: Pulverize almonds in processor with 2 tablespoons flour. Using electric mixer, cream butter and ¼ cup sugar until light and fluffy. Add egg and lemon peel and mix until fluffy. Combine remaining flour and baking powder. Add to butter with almonds, mixing just until blended. Shape dough into 6-inch-long log. Wrap in plastic and refrigerate until firm, at least 1 hour. (*Can be prepared 1 day ahead.*)

Line baking sheets with parchment. Cut dough into 6 1-inch slices. Roll each out between sheets of plastic wrap to 6-inch disc. Turn out onto prepared sheets, removing plastic and spacing 3 inches apart. Fold ½ inch of edge in; pinch to form ½-inch-high border. Refrigerate 15 minutes. (*Can be prepared 1 day ahead. Wrap tightly.*)

Position rack in center of oven and preheat to 400°F. Combine blueberries, 3 tablespoons sugar and 1 teaspoon cornstarch in small bowl. Divide among 3 crusts. Combine raspberries, 3 tablespoons sugar and 1 teaspoon cornstarch; divide among remaining 3 crusts. Bake pastries until edges are light golden brown, 15 to 20 minutes. Serve warm, topped with dollop of whipped cream.

*If unavailable, frozen berries can be substituted. Thaw, drain and then measure 1⅓ cups.

Individual Berry Shortcakes

For a special variation, use a combination of strawberries and raspberries.

6 servings

- 2 pints (generous) strawberries, hulled and halved if large
- ½ cup sugar

Buttermilk Almond Biscuits
- 2¼ cups all purpose flour
- ½ cup sugar
- 1½ teaspoons baking powder
- ¾ teaspoon baking soda
- ¼ teaspoon salt
- 6 tablespoons (¾ stick) well-chilled unsalted butter, cut into 6 pieces

- ⅔ to 1 cup buttermilk
- 1 egg yolk
- ½ teaspoon vanilla
- ⅛ teaspoon almond extract
  Whipping cream
- ⅓ cup sliced almonds
- 1 tablespoon sugar

- 1¼ cups well-chilled whipping cream
- 1 teaspoon vanilla

Combine berries and sugar in medium bowl. Crush some of berries into sugar using back of wooden spoon. Let stand at room temperature until syrup forms, stirring occasionally, at least 1 hour. Chill while making biscuits.

For biscuits: Preheat oven to 425°F. Butter baking sheet. Blend flour, sugar, baking powder, baking soda and salt in processor. Cut in butter until coarse meal forms, using on/off turns. Mix ⅔ cup buttermilk, yolk, ½ teaspoon vanilla and almond extract in measuring cup. With machine running, pour mixture through feed tube. Add enough buttermilk 1 tablespoon at a time to form sticky dough.

Transfer dough to floured sheet of waxed paper. Using floured fingertips, gently pat dough out to thickness of 3/4 inch. Cut into 3- to 3 1/4-inch rounds, using fluted cutter or glass. Transfer to prepared sheet. Gather dough scraps and reroll. Cut additional biscuits. Brush tops of biscuits with cream. Top with almonds and sprinkle with 1 tablespoon sugar. Bake until biscuits are light golden brown, 11 to 14 minutes. Cool on rack 3 minutes.

Whip 1 1/4 cups cream with vanilla to soft peaks. Halve warm biscuits horizontally, using serrated knife. Arrange bottoms on plates. Ladle berries and juices over. Spoon some of whipped cream over berries. Replace tops and serve immediately. Pass remaining whipped cream separately.

Midnight Delights

These bite-size morsels pack a double dose of chocolate chips and cocoa. They are a perfect carry-along dessert.

Makes 4 dozen

Crust
1 3/4 cups all purpose flour
1/3 cup unsweetened cocoa powder
1/4 cup sugar
   Pinch of salt
3/4 cup (1 1/2 sticks) butter, chilled and cut into small pieces
1/3 to 1/2 cup strong coffee, chilled

Filling
12 ounces semisweet chocolate chips, melted
2/3 cup sugar

2 tablespoons (1/4 stick) butter, melted
2 tablespoons milk
2 teaspoons coffee liqueur
2 eggs, room temperature
1/2 cup finely chopped toasted walnuts

For crust: Sift flour, cocoa, sugar and salt into large bowl of electric mixer or processor work bowl. Add butter and blend until consistency of coarse meal. Gradually mix in coffee. Knead dough briefly, then form into log. Wrap in plastic or aluminum foil and refrigerate several hours or overnight.

Lightly grease tiny muffin pans (diameter of top of each cup should be about 1 3/4 inches). Cut the dough into 4 pieces. Working with 1/4 of dough at a time (keep remainder refrigerated), roll dough out into circle slightly less than 1/8 inch thick and 14 to 15 inches in diameter. Cut dough into circles using 3-inch round cutter. Gently press into prepared muffin cups. Repeat with remaining dough. Chill.

For filling: Preheat oven to 350°F. Combine chocolate, sugar, butter, milk and coffee liqueur in medium bowl and blend well. Add eggs and beat until smooth. Stir in chopped walnuts. Place 1 rounded teaspoon of filling into each muffin cup. Bake until filling is set, about 20 to 25 minutes. Let cool in pans 15 minutes. Transfer to wire racks and let cool completely. (*Midnight Delights can be prepared ahead, wrapped tightly and frozen.*)

Indianerkraphen

Save the centers of these hollowed-out cupcakes and serve with ice cream or fruit sauce, or use for a trifle.

Makes 12

Sponge Cakes
- 6 eggs, separated, room temperature
- 1 tablespoon cold water
- 1/2 teaspoon vanilla
- 8 tablespoons sugar
- 1 cup sifted cake flour

- 3/4 cup melted and strained apricot jam

Chocolate Glaze
- 4 ounces unsweetened chocolate, coarsely chopped
- 3 tablespoons solid vegetable shortening
- 1 pound powdered sugar, sifted
- 1/2 cup boiling water
- 1/2 teaspoon almond extract

Whipped Cream Filling
- 1 teaspoon unflavored gelatin
- 1 tablespoon water
- 1 teaspoon vanilla
- 2 cups well-chilled whipping cream
- 1/3 cup powdered sugar

For cakes: Preheat oven to 350°F. Butter twenty-four 2¼-inch-diameter muffin cups. Using electric mixer, beat yolks, water and vanilla until pale yellow and very thick. In another bowl, beat egg whites until soft peaks form. Add sugar 1 tablespoon at a time and beat until stiff but not dry. Gently fold ¼ of whites into yolks to lighten. Pour yolk mixture over remaining whites. Sift in half of flour and fold gently until almost blends. Sift in remaining flour. Fold until just blended.

Spoon batter into prepared tins. Bake until cakes are lightly colored and springy to touch, 10 to 12 minutes. Cool 3 minutes in pans. Loosen sides with spatula, turn out onto racks and cool completely. (*Can be prepared 2 days ahead. Freeze, then wrap tightly. Thaw cakes uncovered at room temperature before continuing.*)

Cut out center of each cake, leaving ⅜-inch shell. Brush outside of each shell with jam. Invert onto sheets of waxed paper. Let dry until outside is no longer sticky, about 40 minutes.

For glaze: Melt chocolate and shortening in top of double boiler set over barely simmering water. Whisk in 1 cup powdered sugar, then boiling water. Add remaining sugar 1 cup at a time, whisking until glaze is smooth. Mix in ½ teaspoon almond extract.

Keep glaze over hot water. Hold cake by spreading fingers inside hollow. Dip outside of cake into glaze to rim. Allow excess glaze to drain back into pan. Invert cake on rack set over waxed paper. Whisk glaze and repeat with remaining cakes. Let stand until glaze is firm, about 30 minutes.

For filling: Soften gelatin in water in small bowl. Set bowl in pan of very hot water and stir until gelatin is dissolved. Stir in vanilla. Using electric mixer, whip cream until soft peaks form. Beat in sugar and gelatin mixture; continue beating until very stiff.

Spoon cream into pastry bag fitted with large star tip. Pipe mixture into hollows of 2 cakes, mounding ½-inch above edges. Press cream-filled sides of cakes together, allowing some cream to encircle center. Repeat with remaining cakes. (*Can be prepared 8 hours ahead and refrigerated. Let stand at room temperature 15 minutes before serving.*)

Blueberry Cheesecake Cookies

These cookies freeze well.

Makes about 4 dozen

1¼ cups graham cracker crumbs
⅓ cup butter, melted
2 tablespoons sugar
2 8-ounce packages cream cheese, room temperature

2 eggs, room temperature
½ cup sugar
1 teaspoon vanilla
1 21-ounce can blueberry pie filling

Preheat oven to 375°F. Place paper liners in miniature muffin tins. Combine graham cracker crumbs, butter and 2 tablespoons sugar in medium bowl and mix thoroughly. Press 1 rounded teaspoon crumb mixture firmly into bottom of each liner. Combine cream cheese, eggs, remaining sugar and vanilla in large bowl. Beat with electric mixer until thoroughly blended, about 4 minutes. Spoon 2 teaspoons cheese mixture into each cup. Bake until firm, about 10 minutes. Let cool about 10 minutes. Top each with 1 teaspoon blueberry pie filling. Refrigerate until ready to serve.

Moravian Sugar Cakes

Moravian breads always include a potato in the dough, which makes them light and delicately textured.

Makes 14

½ cup sugar
2 envelopes dry yeast
⅔ cup warm water (105°F to 115°F)

¾ cup firmly packed light brown sugar
2 teaspoons cinnamon
2¾ cups bread flour
1 3-ounce potato, baked and peeled

½ cup (1 stick) unsalted butter, cut into 4 pieces, room temperature
2 eggs
½ teaspoon salt

¼ cup (½ stick) unsalted butter, melted

Grease large bowl. In small bowl, sprinkle 1 teaspoon sugar and yeast over water; stir to dissolve. Let stand until foamy, about 5 minutes.

Mix brown sugar and cinnamon in processor 5 seconds. Transfer to plastic bag and seal airtight. Blend flour, remaining sugar, potato, ½ cup butter, eggs and salt 5 seconds. With machine running, pour yeast mixture through feed tube and process until sticky batter forms, about 20 seconds. Transfer to prepared bowl. Cover bowl and let batter rise in warm draft-free area until doubled in volume, about 1 hour.

Oil fourteen ½-cup muffin cups. Stir batter down with wooden spoon. Pour scant ¼ cup batter into each cup. Cover with oiled plastic wrap. Let rise in warm draft-free area until doubled in volume, about 40 minutes.

Position rack in center of oven and preheat to 350°F. Brush tops of cakes with melted butter. Sprinkle each with 1 tablespoon brown sugar mixture. Bake until tester inserted in centers comes out clean, about 20 minutes. Cool 5 minutes. Carefully transfer cakes to rack. Serve warm. (*Can be prepared 1 day ahead. Cool and wrap tightly. To reheat, uncover and place on baking sheet in cold oven. Set temperature to 300°F and bake until warm, about 10 minutes.*)

Peanutty Lemon Bites

Makes about 4 dozen

Pastry
- 1 cup sifted all purpose flour
- 6 ounces cream cheese, room temperature
- 3/4 cup (1 1/2 sticks) butter, room temperature
- 1/4 cup chunky peanut butter, room temperature

Filling
- 1 1/2 cups sugar
- 4 eggs, beaten to blend
- 3/4 cup (1 1/2 sticks) butter, melted
- 2 tablespoons fresh lemon juice
- 1 1/2 tablespoons vinegar
- 3 tablespoons finely chopped peanuts

For pastry: Mix flour, cheese, butter, and peanut butter in large bowl using large fork. Pat pastry into ball. Wrap tightly in plastic. Refrigerate 1 hour.

Pinch off 1-inch ball of pastry. Press into bottom and up sides of 2-inch muffin tin. Repeat with remaining pastry. Refrigerate at least 2 hours.

For filling: Combine all ingredients in large bowl in order given and mix well. Fill each pastry shell 3/4 full. Preheat oven to 325°F. Bake until filling is just set, 20 to 25 minutes. Let cool. Gently remove pastries from tins. Serve immediately or store in airtight container.

Date-Nut Jumbles

8 servings

- 3/4 cup sugar
- 2 eggs, beaten to blend
- 2 tablespoons all purpose flour
- 1 teaspoon baking powder
- Dash of salt
- 1 8-ounce package pitted dates, chopped (about 1 1/4 cups)
- 1/2 cup chopped walnuts or pecans
- 1 cup whipping cream, whipped

Preheat oven to 300°F. Grease eight 3-ounce muffin tins. Beat sugar and eggs in large bowl of electric mixer. Mix flour, baking powder and salt in small bowl and add to egg mixture. Stir in dates and nuts. Spoon batter into prepared tins, filling 2/3 full. Bake until browned and set, 40 to 45 minutes. Cool slightly on rack. Remove muffins from tins and break into chunks. Divide among 8 stemmed glasses or compote dishes. Top each with whipped cream and serve.

Cranberry-Hazelnut Phyllo Baskets

Makes 40

Phyllo Baskets
- 8 phyllo pastry sheets
- 20 tablespoons (2 1/2 sticks) unsalted butter, melted
- 6 tablespoons finely ground dry breadcrumbs

Cranberry Topping
- 1 12-ounce package cranberries
- 1 1/2 cups sugar
- 6 tablespoons water

Cream Cheese Filling
- 10 ounces cream cheese, room temperature
- 8 1/2 tablespoons powdered sugar
- 1 1/4 tablespoons grated lemon peel
- 2 1/2 teaspoons fresh lemon juice
- 1/3 cup coarsely chopped toasted husked hazelnuts

For baskets: Place 1 phyllo sheet on work surface. (Cover remaining sheets with damp towel to prevent drying.) Brush with 2 tablespoons melted butter. Sprinkle with 1 tablespoon breadcrumbs. Repeat with 3 more sheets; do not sprinkle fourth sheet with breadcrumbs. Repeat entire process 1 more time for total of 2 stacks of 4 sheets each. Mark off twenty 3-inch squares on each stack using ruler. Cut into squares using scissors or pizza cutter.

Preheat oven to 350°F. Brush 40 miniature muffin cups with remaining butter. Press 1 stacked phyllo square into each muffin cup, forming basket. Bake until lightly browned, 10 to 12 minutes. Cook 5 minutes. Transfer baskets to rack and cool to room temperature. (*Can be prepared 2 weeks ahead. Store at room temperature.*)

For topping: Cook cranberries, sugar and water in heavy medium saucepan over low heat until sugar dissolves, swirling pan occasionally. Increase heat and bring to boil. Reduce heat and cook until berries pop, about 10 minutes. Refrigerate until cool. (*Can be prepared 1 week ahead.*)

For filling: Blend cream cheese and sugar with electric mixer until smooth and creamy. Add peel and juice.

To assemble: Divide cream cheese filling among phyllo baskets, spreading evenly. Spoon about 1 teaspoon cranberry topping over filling. Sprinkle with hazelnuts. (*Can be prepared 4 hours ahead and refrigerated. Bring to room temperature before serving.*)

Chocolate Baklava

This delectable variation on a Greek favorite can be assembled and frozen three months ahead. For best results, bake them the day they will be served.

Makes about 40

Syrup
4½ cups sugar
3 cups water
2 3-inch cinnamon sticks
1 tablespoon fresh lemon juice

Walnut Filling
2½ pounds chopped walnuts
1 teaspoon almond extract

1 pound phyllo pastry sheets
1½ cups (3 sticks) unsalted butter, melted

Paper baking cups
Easy Fudge Sauce*
Additional chopped walnuts

For syrup: Cook all ingredients in heavy large saucepan over low heat, swirling pan occasionally, until sugar dissolves. Increase heat and boil gently 20 minutes. Cool. Discard cinnamon.

For filling: Combine 2½ pounds walnuts, almond extract and 2 cups syrup in large bowl. Add more syrup if necessary to make moist mixture that sticks together. Reserve syrup.

Cut pastry sheets in half crosswise. Brush 1 sheet with butter (keep remainder covered with damp towel). Place 2 tablespoons filling on one short end. Fold long edges over filling. Roll up jelly roll fashion, starting at short end with filling. Arrange seam side down on ungreased baking sheet.

Brush top with butter. Repeat with remaining filling and pastry, spacing pastries 2 inches apart. (*Can be prepared 1 month ahead. Place pastries close together on parchment-lined pan. Cover tightly and freeze. Refrigerate remaining syrup. Before baking, transfer frozen pastries to ungreased baking sheet, spacing 2 inches apart. Do not thaw before baking.*)

Preheat oven to 375°F. Bake pastries until golden brown and crisp, about 20 minutes for room temperature or 30 minutes for frozen. Cool 5 minutes. Brush top of each pastry with some of reserved syrup to glaze. Cool.

Place each pastry on plate. Spoon Easy Fudge Sauce over. Top with walnuts. (*Can be prepared 6 hours ahead.*)

*Easy Fudge Sauce

Makes about 1 cup

1/3 cup butter	1 cup powdered sugar
2 1/2 squares unsweetened chocolate	1/3 cup milk

Melt butter and chocolate in top of double boiler over barely simmering water. Slowly mix in sugar alternately with milk. Cook 20 minutes, stirring occasionally. (*Can be prepared 5 days ahead. Cover and refrigerate. Reheat in top of double boiler before using.*)

Walnut-Filled Pastry Flutes

Makes about 100

Syrup
2 cups plus 3 tablespoons sugar
1 cup water
1 tablespoon fresh lemon juice
1 tablespoon honey
1 3-inch cinnamon stick
3 whole cloves

Filling
3 cups ground walnuts
1 teaspoon cinnamon
1/4 teaspoon ground cloves

2 egg whites, room temperature, beaten to consistency of mayonnaise

1 pound phyllo pastry sheets
1 cup (2 sticks) butter, melted
Powdered sugar

For syrup: Cook all ingredients in heavy medium saucepan over low heat, swirling pan occasionally, until sugar dissolves, then boil 15 minutes. Cool completely; strain.

For filling: Combine walnuts, cinnamon and cloves in mixing bowl. Blend in 1 cup syrup and whites (mixture should not be too stiff; add up to 1/4 cup additional syrup if necessary).

To assemble: Preheat oven to 350°F. Cut phyllo sheets into 5 × 8-inch strips. Cover with plastic until ready to use. Brush one strip lightly with melted butter. Spread 1 heaping teaspoon of filling along narrow edge. Fold in sides 1/2 inch toward center. Brush sides lightly with butter. Roll up tightly. Repeat with remaining phyllo strips and filling. Arrange seam side down on baking sheet. Pour remaining butter over. Bake until golden and crisp, 20 to 25 minutes. Cool completely. Dust lightly with powdered sugar.

Crisp Honey-Nut Spirals

2 servings

3 tablespoons finely chopped walnuts (about 1/2 ounce)
2 teaspoons sugar
Pinch of cinnamon
Pinch of ground cloves
1 phyllo pastry sheet
2 tablespoons (1/4 stick) butter, melted

1 tablespoon sugar
1 tablespoon water
1 tablespoon honey
1 teaspoon fresh lime juice

Preheat oven to 350°F. Mix walnuts, 2 teaspoons sugar, cinnamon and cloves in small bowl. Brush phyllo lightly with melted butter. Cut into quarters. Make 2 stacks of 2 quarters each. Brush each lightly with melted butter. Sprinkle half of nut mixture over each. Using chopstick, roll each up to form cylinder around chopstick. Gently press ends in (pastry should appear gathered). Carefully slide chopstick out. Coil cylinders. Place seam side down on baking sheet with sides touching. Brush with remaining melted butter. Bake until golden brown, 15 to 20 minutes.

Meanwhile, combine remaining sugar, water, honey and lime juice in heavy small saucepan over medium heat and simmer 10 minutes. Transfer spirals to serving dish. Slit tops and pour syrup over. Serve immediately, or let cool and serve at room temperature. (*Can be prepared 2 days ahead, covered tightly and refrigerated.*)

Kadaife with Citrus and Nuts

Kadaife dough, which has the texture of shredded wheat, is used frequently in Greek desserts. In this recipe, it is filled with nuts, orange juice and cinnamon, baked and then dressed with simple syrup. The dough is available at Greek and Middle Eastern markets.

Makes 18 to 20

1 pound kadaife pastry dough	Butter
2 cups minced walnuts or minced blanched almonds	1 cup (2 sticks) unsalted butter, melted and clarified
½ cup fresh orange juice	1½ cups sugar
⅓ cup sugar	1 cup water
1 teaspoon cinnamon	2 teaspoons fresh lemon juice

Open pastry and air dry 15 minutes.

Combine walnuts, orange juice, ⅓ cup sugar and cinnamon in small bowl.

Preheat oven to 350°F. Lightly butter baking sheet. Separate pastry strands. Shape into eighteen to twenty 10- to 12-inch rectangles. Place 1 tablespoon filling at narrow end of rectangle. Roll up tightly as for jelly roll, making sure filling is completely covered. Repeat with remaining pastry and filling. Arrange on prepared baking sheet; do not crowd. Pour melted butter over. Bake until golden, 35 to 40 minutes.

Meanwhile, cook 1½ cups sugar, water and lemon juice in heavy medium saucepan over low heat, swirling pan occasionally, until sugar dissolves, then simmer 15 minutes. Pour hot sugar syrup over pastry. Serve kadaife at room temperature.

Great-Grandma Vratny's Jelly Puffs

Enjoy these light pastries the same day they are cooked. For variety, coat some with cinnamon sugar, others with jelly—and some with both.

Makes about 2 dozen

3 tablespoons sugar	¼ teaspoon grated lemon peel
1 envelope dry yeast	4 cups (about) sifted all purpose flour
1 cup warm milk (105°F to 115°F)	
5 tablespoons butter, room temperature	Vegetable oil (for deep frying)
1 egg, room temperature	½ cup sugar mixed with 2½ tablespoons cinnamon
1 tablespoon vanilla	½ cup raspberry or currant jelly
½ teaspoon salt	
¼ teaspoon freshly grated nutmeg or mace	

Sprinkle sugar and yeast over $^1/_2$ cup warm milk in bowl of heavy-duty electric mixer; stir to dissolve. Let stand until foamy, about 10 minutes.

Add remaining $^1/_2$ cup warm milk, butter, egg, vanilla, salt, nutmeg and lemon peel to yeast and mix until butter melts. Add 2 cups flour and mix with dough hook until smooth. Add enough of remaining flour $^1/_2$ cup at a time to form slightly sticky but somewhat firm dough. Mix until dough is smooth and blisters form on surface, about 10 minutes. (Dough can also be mixed and kneaded by hand.) Place dough in large bowl. Sprinkle top with flour. Cover bowl with towel. Let dough rise in warm draft-free area until doubled, about 1½ hours.

Flour baking sheets. Gently pat dough out on lightly floured surface to thickness of $^1/_2$ inch. Cut out 2-inch circles, using floured cookie cutter or glass. Transfer rounds to prepared sheets. Gather scraps together and knead until smooth. Pat out dough to thickness of $^1/_2$ inch and cut additional rounds. Cover with towel. Let rise in warm area until doubled, about 1 hour.

Heat 1 inch oil in large skillet to 375°F. Add rounds in batches (do not crowd) and cook until golden brown, about 2 minutes on each side. Drain on paper towels. Cool to warm or room temperature. Just before serving, roll some in cinnamon sugar and spread 1 teaspoon jelly atop others.

Fruit Doughnuts with Berry Sauce

For a cooling counterpoint, place a scoop of vanilla ice cream in each bowl before adding doughnuts.

4 servings

Sauce
- 1 pound raspberries or strawberries
- 1 cup sugar
- $^3/_4$ cup water

Doughnuts (makes 20)
- 1$^3/_4$ cups all purpose flour
- 1 cup mashed cooked baking potato
- $^1/_2$ cup sugar
- 1 egg
- 1$^1/_2$ tablespoons baking powder
- $^1/_2$ teaspoon vanilla
- $^1/_2$ teaspoon cinnamon (optional)
- $^1/_3$ cup buttermilk
- 1$^1/_4$ cups diced strawberries
- $^1/_3$ cup chopped walnuts
- $^1/_3$ cup dried currants

Vegetable oil (for deep frying)

Powdered sugar

For sauce: Heat all ingredients in heavy large saucepan over low heat until sugar dissolves, swirling pan occasionally. Increase heat and bring to boil. Reduce heat and simmer 5 minutes. Cool completely. Puree in processor. Strain to eliminate seeds. Refrigerate sauce until ready to serve.

For doughnuts: Mix flour, potato, sugar, egg, baking powder, vanilla and cinnamon (if desired) in large bowl. Gradually blend in buttermilk. Stir in berries, walnuts and currants.

Heat 6 inches of oil in deep fryer or heavy deep saucepan to 350°F. Drop batter into oil by heaping tablespoons (do not crowd). Fry until browned and crisp (interior will be soft), about 4 minutes. Remove doughnuts from oil using slotted spoon. Drain on paper towels. Let stand 3 minutes to firm.

Divide doughnuts evenly among plates or bowls. Sprinkle some with powdered sugar. Spoon sauce over remainder. Serve immediately.

Fruit and Nut Strudel

Fruit and Nut Strudel freezes well.

Makes 4 strudels

2 cups all purpose flour, sifted
1 cup (2 sticks) well-chilled butter
1 cup chilled sour cream

1¹/₃ cups apricot preserves
1¹/₃ cups raisins

1¹/₃ cups chopped walnuts
Powdered sugar

Place flour in large bowl. Cut in butter using pastry blender or two knives until mixture resembles coarse meal. Stir in sour cream and mix to form dough. Flatten dough into disc. Wrap in waxed paper. Refrigerate overnight.

Preheat oven to 375°F. Divide chilled dough into 4 equal portions. Roll each section out on floured surface into thin rectangle about 12 × 4 inches. Drop spoonfuls of preserves onto dough, spreading evenly. Sprinkle raisins and nuts evenly over top. Roll rectangles up lengthwise as for jelly roll. Transfer to baking sheet. Bake until golden brown, about 45 minutes. Let cool on racks. Cut into ¹/₂- to ³/₄-inch slices. Sprinkle with powdered sugar.

Mae Goodman's Hungarian Coffee Crescents

These are a perfect, not-too-sweet accompaniment to coffee.

Makes 48 crescents

Pastry
3 cups all purpose flour
3 tablespoons sugar
1 cup (2 sticks) well-chilled unsalted butter
3 egg yolks, beaten
2 envelopes dry yeast or 2 cakes fresh yeast dissolved in ¹/₂ cup lukewarm milk
1¹/₂ teaspoons vanilla

Filling
3 egg whites, room temperature
²/₃ cup sugar

¹/₂ cup sugar
2 teaspoons cinnamon
¹/₂ cup ground walnuts or pecans

1 egg beaten with 2 teaspoons water
Powdered sugar (optional garnish)

For pastry: Combine dry ingredients in processor or bowl. Cut in butter until mixture resembles coarse meal. Add yolks, yeast mixture and vanilla and blend until combined. Wrap tightly and refrigerate overnight.

Remove dough from refrigerator and divide into 6 equal pieces.

For filling: Beat egg whites until stiff peaks form. Gradually beat in ²/₃ cup sugar. Combine remaining sugar with cinnamon and nuts.

Grease baking sheets or use heavy-duty foil. Roll out 1 piece of dough into very thin round on lightly floured surface. Brush with egg white and then sprinkle with some of nut mixture. Using sharp knife, cut into 8 equal wedges. Starting at large end, roll wedges up, shaping gently into crescent. Transfer to prepared sheets or foil, spacing about 2 inches apart. Repeat with remaining dough. Let stand at room temperature 30 minutes to rise.

Preheat oven to 350°F. Lightly brush each crescent with beaten egg. Bake until crisp and pale gold, about 20 minutes. Let cool on wire rack. Dust with powdered sugar before serving.

If baking crescents ahead, let cool, wrap tightly and freeze. Defrost in refrigerator the day before serving. Crisp in 350°F oven on day of party. When cool, arrange on serving platter and cover lightly; do not return to refrigerator.

Index

🍎 Credits and Acknowledgments

The following people contributed the recipes included in this book:

Laura Lee Alpert
Jean Anderson
Sandi Anderson
John and Dee Andronico
Reza Asadi
Pamella Asquith
Nancy Baggett
Nancy Barr
Joan and Wade Baxley
Bear's Brown Bag, Lake Arrowhead,
   California
Freddi Bercovitch
Lena Birnbaum
Adrienne Blocker
Carol Bowen
Martha Buller
Carol Chabot
Don and Molly Chappellet
Pat Connell
Ruth Crassweller
Diane Darrow
Connie De Brenes
Alice Selby Douglas
Ann Drabkin
Claudia Ebeling
Mary Ernst
Olivia Erschen
Selma Estrem
Rodney Eubanks
Joe Famularo
Sherry Ferguson
Carol Field
Helen Fletcher
Foothill House, Calistoga, California
Frankenmuth Bavarian Inn,
   Frankenmuth, Michigan
Lynn Friss
Lee Gardner
Debra Josephs Givon
Peggy Glass
Dorothy Gonzales
Lorraine Warren Gooze
Julie Gordon
Marion Gorman
Freddi Greenberg

Rhonda Gritzmacher
Penny Gusack
Betsy Harker
Raina Harris
Ethel Hornbeck
Barbara Horowitz
Janet Hurst
Beverly Jackson
Madeleine Kamman
Cyndee Kannenberg
Barbara Karoff
Lynne Kasper
Sharon Katz
Sotiris Kitrilakis
Diane and Jim Kronman
Alyse Laemmle
Lynne Lang
Anne Marie Latimer
Mei Lee
Clara Less
Faye Levy
Ina Lieb
Mainstay Inn, Cape Main, New Jersey
Abby Mandel
Pamela Manning
Tom Maresca
Christina McClure
Berenice McLaughlin
Jacqueline McMahan
Miriam Miller
Aline Mobley
Jefferson and Jinx Morgan
Selma Morrow
Beatrice Ojakangas
Lori Openden
Marsha Palanci
Peter's Palate Pleaser Inc., Birmingham,
   Michigan
Jane Palmer
Daniel Pannebaker
Kathryn Pease
Sara Perry
Martha Peters
Vicki Pierson
Fern Pietruszka

Marcia Pilgeram
Alison Poccia
Pat Porter
Marcy Goldman-Posluns
Thelma Pressman
Carolyn Reagan
John Reaves
Joyce Resnik
Marysol Richwine
Elizabeth Riely
Michael Roberts
Betty Rosbottom
Nancy Rosen
Arlene and Lou Sarappo
Richard Sax
Susan Seitz
Dee Sheinbein
Edena Sheldon
Judy Sherman
Elsie Silva
Nina Simonds
Shirley Slater
Clarice Slover
Some Crust Bakery, Claremont,
   California
Southern Hills Country Club, Tulsa,
   Oklahoma
Douglas Singler
Anne Stewart
Pat Tanner
Teresa's Place, Jackson, California
Marimar Torres
Michele Urvater
Nancy Ellard Vass
Carol Lee Veitch
Morag Walker
Jan Weimer
Windows on the World, New York,
   New York
Jo-Ann Zbytniewski
Alan Zeman

Additional text was supplied by: Jan
Weimer and Joyce Resnik, *Pointers for
Perfect Cookies;* Faye Levy, *Macaroons.*

Special thanks to:

Editorial Staff:
   Angeline Vogl
   Mary Jane Bescoby

Graphics Staff:
   Bernard Rotondo
   Gloriane Harris

Rights and Permissions:
   Karen Legier

Indexer:
   Rose Grant

The Knapp Press
is a wholly owned subsidiary of Knapp Communications Corporation

Composition by Andresen's Tucson Typographic Service, Inc., Tucson, Arizona

This book is set in Sabon, a face designed by Jan Teischold
in 1967 and based on early fonts engraved by Garamond and Granjon.